World War II in Europe

Philip Gavin
AR B.L.: 10.3 Alt.: 1516
Points: 6.0   UG

WORLD
HISTORY SERIES

World War II in Europe

Titles in the World History Series

WORLD HISTORY SERIES ■ ■ ■

World War II in Europe

by
Philip Gavin

LUCENT
BOOKS®

THOMSON
★
GALE ™

San Diego • Detroit • New York • San Francisco • Cleveland • New Haven, Conn. • Waterville, Maine • London • Munich

THOMSON
GALE

For more information, contact
Lucent Books
27500 Drake Rd.
Farmington Hills, MI 48331-3535
Or you can visit our Internet site at http://www.gale.com

LIBRARY OF CONGRESS CATALOGING-IN-PUBLICATION DATA

Gavin, Philip.
    World war II in Europe / by Philip Gavin.
      p. cm. — (World history series)
Includes bibliographical references and index.
    ISBN 1-59018-185-9 (alk. paper)
    1. World War, 1939–1945—Juvenile literature. 2. Germany—Politics and government—1933–1945—Juvenile literature. 3. Hitler, Adolf, 1889–1945—Juvenile literature.
I. Title. II. Title: World War II in Europe. III. Title: World War 2 in Europe. IV. Series.
    D756.G28 2004
    940.54'21—dc22
                                                                        2004010209

Printed in the United States of America

Contents

Foreword

Each year on the first day of school, nearly every history teacher faces the task of explaining why his or her students should study history. One logical answer to this question is that exploring what happened in our past explains how the things we often take for granted—our customs, ideas, and institutions—came to be. As statesman and historian Winston Churchill put it, "Every nation or group of nations has its own tale to tell. Knowledge of the trials and struggles is necessary to all who would comprehend the problems, perils, challenges, and opportunities which confront us today." Thus, a study of history puts modern ideas and institutions in perspective. For example, though the founders of the United States were talented and creative thinkers, they clearly did not invent the concept of democracy. Instead, they adapted some democratic ideas that had originated in ancient Greece and with which the Romans, the British, and others had experimented. An exploration of these cultures, then, reveals their very real connection to us through institutions that continue to shape our daily lives.

Another reason often given for studying history is the idea that lessons exist in the past from which contemporary societies can benefit and learn. This idea, although controversial, has always been an intriguing one for historians. Those who agree that society can benefit from the past often quote philosopher George Santayana's famous statement, "Those who cannot remember the past are condemned to repeat it." Historians who subscribe to Santayana's philosophy believe that, for example, studying the events that led up to the major world wars or other significant historical events would allow society to chart a different and more favorable course in the future.

Just as difficult as convincing students of the importance of studying history is the search for useful and interesting supplementary materials that present historical events in a context that can be easily understood. The volumes in Lucent Books' World History Series attempt to present a broad, balanced, and penetrating view of the march of history. Ancient Egypt's important wars and rulers, for example, are presented against the rich and colorful backdrop of Egyptian religious, social, and cultural developments. The series engages the reader by enhancing historical events with these cultural contexts. For example, in *Ancient Greece*, the text covers the role of women in that society. Slavery is discussed in *The Roman Empire*, as well as how slaves earned their freedom. The numerous and varied aspects of everyday life in these and other societies are explored in each volume of the series. Additionally, the series covers the major political, cultural, and philosophical ideas as the torch of civilization is passed from ancient Mesopotamia and Egypt, through Greece, Rome, Medieval Europe, and other world cultures, to the modern day.

The material in the series is formatted in a thorough, precise, and organized manner. Each volume offers the reader a comprehensive and clearly written overview of an important historical event or period. The topic under discussion is placed in a broad, historical context. For example, *The Italian Renaissance* begins with a discussion of the High Middle Ages and the loss of central control that allowed certain Italian cities to develop artistically. The book ends by looking forward to the Reformation and interpreting the societal changes that grew out of the Renaissance. Thus, students are not only involved in an historical era, but also enveloped by the events leading up to that era and the events following it.

One important and unique feature in the World History Series is the primary and secondary source quotations that richly supplement each volume. These quotes are useful in a number of ways. First, they allow students access to sources they would not normally be exposed to because of the difficulty and obscurity of the original source. The quotations range from interesting anecdotes to farsighted cultural perspectives and are drawn from historical witnesses both past and present. Second, the quotes demonstrate how and where historians themselves derive their information on the past as they strive to reach a consensus on historical events. Lastly, all of the quotes are footnoted, familiarizing students with the citation process and allowing them to verify quotes and/or look up the original source if the quote piques their interest.

Finally, the books in the World History Series provide a detailed launching point for further research. Each book contains a bibliography specifically geared toward student research. A second, annotated bibliography introduces students to all the sources the author consulted when compiling the book. A chronology of important dates gives students an overview, at a glance, of the topic covered. Where applicable, a glossary of terms is included.

In short, the series is designed not only to acquaint readers with the basics of history, but also to make them aware that their lives are a part of an ongoing human saga. Perhaps then they will come to the same realization as famed historian Arnold Toynbee. In his monumental work, *A Study of History*, he wrote about becoming aware of history flowing through him in a mighty current, and of his own life "welling like a wave in the flow of this vast tide."

IMPORTANT DATES DURING WORLD WAR II IN EUROPE

July 29, 1921
Adolf Hitler becomes leader of the Nazi Party.

November 11, 1918
World War I ends with Germany's defeat.

September 1, 1939
Hitler invades Poland.

March 16, 1935
Hitler violates the Treaty of Versailles by introducing mandatory enlistment for Germans.

November 9–10, 1938
Kristallnacht, the "Night of Broken Glass" occurs as Nazis stage a national riot targeting Jews.

September 3, 1939
Britain, France, Australia, and New Zealand declare war on Germany.

1920	1932	1934	1936	1938	1940

June 28, 1919
Victorious Allies of World War I, including Britain and France, sign the punitive Treaty of Versailles targeting Germany.

January 30, 1933
Capitalizing on Germany's misfortune, Adolf Hitler is appointed chancellor, bringing the Nazis to power.

September 15, 1935
German Jews become noncitizens via the Nuremberg Laws.

March 7, 1936
Hitler's troops occupy the Rhineland area bordering France.

March 13, 1938
Hitler announces Austria is now part of Nazi Germany.

April 9, 1940
Nazis invade Denmark and Norway.

May 10, 1940
Nazis invade France, Belgium, Luxembourg, and the Netherlands.

July 10, 1940
The Battle of Britain air war begins.

July 1941
Nazi SS troops
begin mass murder
in occupied Russia.

May 13, 1943
German troops in North
Africa surrender to the
British and Americans.

April 30, 1945
Adolf Hitler commits
suicide in his Berlin
bunker. German forces
surrender unconditionally
to the Allies 7 days later.

June 22, 1941
Germany invades
Soviet Russia.

June 6, 1944
D-day
landings in
northern
France open a
new front
against Hitler.

November 20, 1945
Nuremberg war
crime trials begin
for high-ranking
Nazis.

December 8, 1941
The United States
and Britain declare
war on Japan.

| 1942 | 1943 | 1944 | 1945 | 1990 |

December 11, 1941
Hitler declares war on
the United States. The
United States then
declares war on
Germany.

August 25, 1944
Paris is liberated
after four years of
Nazi occupation.

April 29, 1945
The U.S.
Seventh
Army
liberates
Dachau.

January 1942
Mass murder of Jews
by gassing begins at
Auschwitz in occupied
Poland.

January 27, 1945
Russian troops
liberate Auschwitz
where millions
perished.

October 3, 1990
After forty-five
years apart, East
and West
Germany are
reunified as the
Federal Republic
of Germany.

February 2, 1943
German Sixth Army
surrenders at Stalingrad.

April 21, 1945
The Russian army
reaches Berlin.

Legacy of Destruction

At dawn on Friday, September 1, 1939, a massive German army, obeying the orders of its supreme commander, Adolf Hitler, invaded neighboring Poland, smashing everything in sight. This unprovoked attack by Nazi Germany marked the beginning of a six-year war in Europe that became history's most lethal conflict, costing almost 50 million lives.

The people of Germany, beset by staggering economic and political problems in the 1920s and early 1930s, had chosen to blindly follow a dynamic leader who promised to improve their lives and restore Germany to greatness. However, after achieving total power in Germany, Hitler instead pursued his own deadly agenda which included the conquest of Europe and Russia and mass exterminations of unwanted persons, especially Jews.

Remarkably, most Germans were not in favor of Hitler's new war. Two decades earlier, they had endured devastating losses of life as German armies tried but failed to conquer Western Europe in what became known as World War I. However, when Hitler announced in 1939 they were

at war again, they went along with their führer (supreme leader) and were delighted as Hitler's troops roared across Europe, taking country after country with seeming ease.

UNPRECEDENTED MAGNITUDE

The outbreak of World War II in September 1939 challenged all notions of traditional warfare. Most previous European wars were mainly fought along traditional lines on rural battlegrounds away from heavily populated areas. This allowed armies much room to maneuver, minimized the civilian death toll, and preserved Europe's cultural and architectural heritage. But during World War II, civilian populations were no longer exempt from the consequences of war. Indeed, they were even targeted by Hitler's invading armies and air force to create panic and mass confusion, thereby weakening the ability of their military and government leaders to respond.

Above all, civilians fleeing the advancing German army feared Hitler's fighter planes. They would appear seemingly out of nowhere and machine-gun helpless families along congested roadways, then disappear, leaving a trail of agony behind. For those who survived, and for the rest of Europe's civilian population, the unavoidable conquest of their country by Hitler meant an instant loss of freedom as a Nazi police state was swiftly imposed, with severe penalties for anyone who offended the new rulers.

When Hitler tried to extend his empire into Russia beginning in June 1941, he considered the killing of civilians there to be a vital element in his overall strategy for victory. Obeying the orders of their leader, German armed forces and security units thus engaged in the murder of civilians on an unprecedented scale.

IMMORAL MORALITY

Although they were citizens of a country with a notable list of past philosophers, scholars, and writers, followers of Adolf Hitler turned away from traditional notions of right and wrong. They adopted an absolutist mentality crafted by Hitler in which stronger, supposedly superior humans were destined, even obligated, to dominate and destroy the weak.

German children were drilled to believe it was their sacred duty to obey without question *all* orders from above. Members of the military and civilian workers each swore an oath of personal obedience to Hitler. Obedience itself came to assume an aura of holiness in Nazi Germany, so that when the order was

French townspeople flee with their possessions during a Nazi air raid. Nazi fighter planes deliberately targeted civilian populations, often machine-gunning families as they fled.

Human remains are visible in the crematoria ovens at the Buchenwald concentration camp. Adolf Hitler established such camps as part of his systematic plan to exterminate Jews and others.

given to invade a country or assassinate helpless civilians, it was promptly carried out.

For Hitler, and thus for the German people, victory was all that mattered. To achieve that victory, they would willingly sacrifice their own lives, or take countless lives whenever it was deemed necessary by a superior authority. Europe and Russia were therefore subjected to a reign of terror in which human life was not valued.

HITLER'S GREATEST FOE

By the summer of 1941, Hitler was indeed on the verge of victory, ruling an empire that stretched from Paris to the outskirts of Moscow. However, in attacking Soviet Russia, Hitler had taken on Josef Stalin, a ruthless dictator like himself who did not value human life. This set the stage for a mammoth struggle between two all-powerful and determined tyrants that would decide the future of Europe, and the world.

Time after time, Hitler and Stalin pitted all of their available human and material resources against each other at places such as Stalingrad and Kursk. Eighty percent of all German military casualties suffered in World War II would occur at the hands of Russian soldiers, who fought and died by the millions. Stalin was willing to send an unlimited number of young men to their deaths to defeat Hitler's armies. For Stalin, as for Hitler, victory was all that mattered. At Stalingrad alone a million Russians perished during a battle inside the city that for a time seemed hopeless. All over Russia, German officers watched in amazement as their troops mowed down wave upon wave of attackers, only to see new waves appear and attack again.

For Hitler, the unyielding Russian opposition spelled disaster. Faced with a limited supply of soldiers and weapons of war, Hitler had hoped for a swift victory in Russia, similar to his string of lightning-fast conquests throughout Europe. Instead, he found himself drawn into a bloodfest that would last years, decimating the German army and paving the way for the Americans and British invasion of Western Europe.

Wasted Lives

The contemplation of defeat caused Hitler to adopt an extremist attitude toward his perceived enemies and toward the German people themselves. He became willing to send countless young soldiers to their deaths to sustain a conflict that became more hopeless with each passing day. In addition, Hitler was incited to murderous rage against the Jews of Europe, who, according to his twisted logic, were somehow responsible for the disastrous war which he himself had started. Thus he sent them to their deaths by the millions.

An entire continent was turned upside down by one man, Adolf Hitler, totally interrupting life's normal pursuits. Instead of sitting in a classroom or working in a shop, the young men of Europe and Russia found themselves shooting, bombing, and beating each other to death. Instead of playing ball or studying the Torah, young Jews found themselves stuffed in boxcars, headed for the gas chamber. A terrible darkness had descended across the continent, and in its shadow the light of joy, hope, and positive human potential was for a time diminished.

1 The Rise of Hitler

By the beginning of the twentieth century, Germany had become one of the world's great military powers and also a main player in the colossal conflict known as World War I. Amid cheering war rallies, eager young men throughout Europe and England signed up for what they thought would be a grand military adventure. In reality, they fought and died by the millions as new technologies, including planes, tanks, machine guns, long-range artillery, and deadly gas, were used with lethal precision. Despite their sacrifice, a hopeless stalemate developed along a long line of entrenched fortifications stretching in western Europe from the North Sea, all the way through France into Germany. In these muddy, lice-infested trenches, Adolf Hitler became acquainted with war.

HITLER IN WORLD WAR I

Serving as a dispatch runner, Corporal Hitler rushed messages back and forth between the German command staff in the rear to fighting units on the battlefield. Fellow soldiers regarded Hitler as too eager to please his superiors, but generally a likable loner, notable for his luck avoiding injury and for his bravery.

Hitler's luck ran out after two years of nonstop warfare, when he was wounded in the leg by a shell fragment. He was sent back to Germany to recuperate. Following his recovery, he was assigned to light duty in Munich. Touring the city, Hitler was appalled at the widespread apathy of German civilians toward the war. He also witnessed antiwar demonstrations staged by political radicals known as Marxists. He came to believe that the heroic efforts of German troops were being undermined by disloyal civilians, many of whom Hitler thought were Jewish (deep-rooted prejudices led Hitler to assume this).

Disgusted with the atmosphere in Munich, Hitler returned to the battlefront in March 1917. However, the tide of war had turned and German morale was collapsing. In the final weeks of the war, Hitler was injured during a gas attack which left him temporarily blind. He was sent back to Germany, a country now on the verge of anarchy with Marxist agitators roaming the streets and calling for revolution.

Amid the turmoil, Hitler lay helpless in a hospital bed. On November 10, 1918, an elderly pastor entered the hospital ward and announced the news: Germany had surrendered. The war was over.

Years later, Hitler recalled his reaction: "There followed terrible days and even worse nights. . . . In these nights hatred grew in me, hatred for those responsible for this deed."[1] For the rest of his life, Hitler maintained that Germany had not been defeated on the battlefield but had given up due to the efforts of disloyal civilians and defeatist politicians who preferred to end the war. The consequences of Germany's surrender soon became apparent.

THE TREATY OF VERSAILLES

Flushed with victory, representatives from Britain, France, the United States, and other Allied nations who had defeated Germany gathered in Versailles, France, to determine Germany's postwar fate.

On June 28, 1919, they signed the Treaty of Versailles, designed to prevent future German aggression. The treaty forced Germany to accept sole responsibility for causing World War I and required the payment of billions in war reparations. Germany also had to yield borderland areas to neighboring France and Poland. In addition, the German army was reduced to one hundred thousand soldiers and prohibited from obtaining new weapons.

Such punitive measures, however, had unintended consequences. The once-proud German nation stood humiliated before the whole world, creating a passionate desire in many Germans to see their nation rise again. The treaty also imposed a financial burden that delayed Germany's postwar economic recovery, generating major political instability.

Adolf Hitler (seated, far left) served as a corporal in the German army during World War I. Following Germany's humiliating defeat, Hitler vowed to return the nation to glory.

UNSTABLE DEMOCRACY

Germany's wartime leader, Kaiser Wilhelm, had given up the throne upon defeat. Germany then became a democratic republic, a form of government new to Germans. Germany's new democratic leaders crafted a constitution that made the fledgling republic, on paper at least, one of the world's most liberal democracies. However, from the moment it was founded, the new government faced serious opposition from several groups, including ultraconservative ex-soldiers who had supported the kaiser.

Meanwhile, Germany's democratic leaders ratified the Treaty of Versailles. To appease the all-powerful Allies, they abided by the treaty's punitive measures. Their submissive posture caused a growing number of Germans to regard the fledgling democratic government as weak and unworthy of their support. As a result, many antidemocratic movements sprouted across Germany, including a tiny group known as the German Workers' Party. In September 1919 this group eagerly recruited Adolf Hitler.

THE GERMAN WORKERS' PARTY

The German Workers' Party that Hitler stumbled upon in 1919 was a far cry from the immensely powerful, gigantic political organization it would one day become. The first meeting Hitler attended was held in the back room of a Munich beer hall with about twenty-five people in attendance. Hitler, still a member of the German army, had actually been sent by his superiors to investigate this group. The use of the term "workers" sounded Marxist and thus attracted the attention of anti-Marxist army officials.

Although unimpressed by the insignificant German Workers' Party, which had few members and no resources, Hitler sensed the opportunity to mold this struggling political group into a national movement. Invited to join, he thought it over for two days, then concluded, "I had to take this step. . . . It was the most decisive resolve of my life. From here, there was and could be, no turning back."[2] Hitler joined the German Workers' Party (Deutsche Arbeiterpartei or DAP) and thus entered politics.

NAZI PARTY FORMED

After joining the party in September 1919 at age thirty, Hitler immediately began a frenzied effort to make it succeed. The party at this time consisted mainly of an executive committee with seven members, including Hitler. His first idea was to attract new members to the monthly public meeting by sending out invitations and placing newspaper ads. These efforts paid off as about a hundred people showed up for the next meeting.

Hitler was scheduled to be the second speaker at this meeting. He astounded everyone with a highly emotional, at times nearly hysterical manner of speaking. "I spoke for thirty minutes," Hitler later recalled, "and what before I had simply felt within me, without in any way knowing it, was now proved by reality: I could speak! After thirty minutes the people in the small room were electrified and the enthusiasm was first expressed by the . . . donation of three hundred marks [German currency]."[3]

Hitler's Sense of Mission

After the failed Beer Hall Rebellion of November 1923, Hitler was charged with treason by the German government. As his trial concluded, he sensed his growing influence and gave this prophetic closing statement, excerpted from The Face of the Third Reich: Portraits of the Nazi Leadership *by Joachim C. Fest:*

"The man who is born to be a dictator is not compelled. He wills it. He is not driven forward, but drives himself. There is nothing immodest about this. Is it immodest for a worker to drive himself toward heavy labor? Is it presumptuous of a man with the high forehead of a thinker to ponder through the nights till he gives the world an invention? The man who feels called upon to govern a people has no right to say, 'If you want me or summon me, I will cooperate.' No! It is his duty to step forward. The army [of Nazi followers] which we have now formed is growing day to day. I nourish the proud hope that one day the hour will come when these rough companies will grow to battalions, the battalions to regiments, the regiments to divisions, that the old cockade [military ornaments] will be taken from the mud, that the old flags will wave again, that there will be a reconciliation at the last great divine judgment which we are prepared to face."

Hitler believed it was his destiny to control the German people as a dictator.

That money was used to buy more advertising and print leaflets.

From this point onward, the German Workers' Party featured Hitler as its main attraction. In his speeches, Hitler repeated the same themes over and over. He railed against Germany's acceptance of the Treaty of Versailles and delivered anti-Jewish tirades, blaming German Jews for the nation's misfortunes. Attendance steadily increased.

At one meeting in February 1920, before two thousand people, Hitler announced the Twenty-five Points of the German Workers' Party, its political platform. The platform rejected the Treaty of

Versailles outright and advocated a non-democratic style of government. The platform also included the demand for additional territories for the German people and maintained that citizenship should be determined by race, with no Jew considered to be a German. Hitler

In a 1933 ceremony, Nazi officials consecrate the party's flag bearing the swastika, an ancient symbol long used by anti-Semitic political parties in Germany.

later recalled his impression of this first mass meeting:

> When, after nearly four hours, the hall began to empty and the crowd, shoulder to shoulder, began to move, shove, press toward the exit like a slow stream, I knew that now the principles of a movement which could no longer be forgotten were moving out among the German people. . . . A fire was kindled from whose flame one day the sword must come which would regain freedom . . . and life for the German nation.[4]

Hitler realized the movement lacked a recognizable symbol or flag. In the summer of 1920, Hitler chose the symbol which, to this day, is perhaps the most infamous in history—the swastika. It is not something Hitler invented, but is found even in the ruins of ancient times, and had been seen around Germany before as an emblem used by anti-Semitic political parties. It had also appeared among the ultraconservative *Freikorps* (former World War I soldiers) who roamed the streets, putting down Marxist rebellions.

Hitler's striking design placed a black swastika inside a white circle on a red background, providing a powerful, instantly recognizable symbol. Hitler explained the symbolism: "In red we see the social idea of the movement, in white the nationalistic idea, in the swastika the mission of the struggle for the victory of Aryan [Germanic] man, and . . . the victory of the idea of creative work, which as such always has been and always will be anti-Semitic."[5]

Hitler also expanded the German Workers' Party name to include the term National Socialist. Thus the full name became the National Socialist German Workers' Party (Nationalsozialistische Deutsche Arbeiterpartei or NSDAP), popularly called Nazi for short.

HITLER'S FAME GROWS

The Nazi Party was based in Munich, a hotbed of radical politics. By the end of 1920, the party had about three thousand members, including many alienated, maladjusted ex-soldiers with a strong disdain for the Treaty of Versailles and the democratic German government that abided by it. They looked toward the rising politician, Adolf Hitler, and the growing Nazi movement as an alternative and brought in new recruits.

As the Nazi Party gained popularity and public meetings grew, Hitler hoped to seize the momentum and spread his movement to the rest of Germany. Remarkably, a series of financial events soon unfolded, providing great opportunity. In April 1921 two of the victorious allies of World War I, France and England, presented a bill to Germany demanding the equivalent of $33 billion in war reparations. This demand caused instant havoc in Germany's economy by generating ruinous inflation.

The German currency, the mark, slipped drastically in value. Before the reparation demands, four marks equaled one U.S. dollar. After the demands were announced, the mark's value dropped to seventy-five to the dollar and in 1922 sank

to four hundred. By July 1923, it plunged to 160,000. By August, it was a million. And by November 1923, 4 billion marks equaled a single dollar. As a result, Germans lost their life savings. Salaries were paid in worthless paper money. Groceries cost billions. Hunger riots broke out. Antidemocratic agitators throughout Germany clamored for action.

By now, the Nazis, with fifty-five thousand followers, were the biggest militant group in the State of Bavaria. Given the unstable political climate in Germany, radical members of the party felt the time had come to grab power by force and urged Hitler to act.

THE BEER HALL REBELLION

To take over Germany, Hitler and his top aides hatched a complicated plot to kidnap the leaders of the Bavarian government and force them at gunpoint to accept him as their leader. Then, according to the plan, with the support of famous World War I general Erich Ludendorff, they would win over the entire German army, proclaim a nationwide revolt, and bring down the German democratic government in Berlin.

On November 8, 1923, the plan went into action as armed Nazis, under the command of Hermann Göring, surrounded a Munich beer hall where a large business meeting was being held with the government leaders in attendance. Hitler, accompanied by several armed Nazis, burst into the beer hall and fired a pistol shot into the ceiling, shouting, "The National Revolution has begun!"[6] He then ordered the three highest officials of the Bavarian government into a back room and informed them they were to join him in proclaiming a Nazi revolution.

But to Hitler's dismay, the three men refused to talk to him. On a sudden impulse, Hitler dashed out of the room, went up to the podium, and shouted something that implied the prestigious men in the back room had joined his revolution. Wild cheering erupted for Hitler who, choked with emotion, spoke to the crowd:

> I am going to fulfill the vow I made to myself five years ago when I was a blind cripple in the military hospital— to know neither rest nor peace until the November criminals [German politicians who ended World War I] had been overthrown, until on the ruins of the wretched Germany of today there should have arisen once more a Germany of power and greatness, of freedom and splendor.[7]

The crowd roared its approval and sang the German anthem, "Deutschland über Alles." Hitler was euphoric. It appeared he might soon be the new leader of Germany. But then word arrived that attempts by armed Nazis to take over several army barracks had failed and that soldiers inside those barracks were resisting. Hitler decided to leave the beer hall to resolve the problem personally.

Leaving the beer hall was a fateful error. In his absence the three Bavarian government officials slipped away. Meanwhile, Hitler had no luck in getting the German soldiers in the barracks to surrender. Having failed at that, he returned to the beer hall, only to find his entire revolution fizzling.

Hitler stayed up all night, frantically trying to decide what to do next. General Ludendorff, by his side throughout the ordeal, gave him an idea. The Nazis would simply march into the middle of Munich and take over the city. Hitler, now desperate for any idea, agreed to give it a try.

Thus, around 11 A.M. on November 9, 1923, a column of three thousand Nazis, led by Hitler, Göring, and Ludendorff, marched toward the center of Munich. There they encountered one hundred armed policemen forming a blockade. Hitler called for their surrender. Shots rang out. Sixteen Nazis and three policemen were killed. Hitler suffered a dislocated shoulder when the man he had locked arms with was shot and pulled him down to the pavement. Hitler then crawled along the sidewalk, out of the line of fire, and scooted into a waiting car, leaving his comrades behind. The rest of the Nazis scattered or were arrested. For two days, Hitler hid in the attic of a friend's home but was arrested himself. The Nazi revolution, it seemed, had come to a crashing end.

WORLDWIDE NOTORIETY

To most observers, it appeared that Hitler's political career and the threat of Nazi extremism was over. In reality, however, the Beer Hall Rebellion and Hitler's subsequent trial for treason marked the true beginning of his rise to power. Overnight, Hitler became a nationally and internationally known figure due to massive press coverage of the sensational trial. The judges, who were Nazi sympathizers, allowed Hitler to use the courtroom as a propaganda platform from which he could speak at any length on his own behalf, interrupt others at any time, and even cross-examine witnesses.

A group of Nazis stand in front of a barricade during the Munich Beer Hall Rebellion of 1923. The rebellion was quickly put down, and Hitler and the Nazis were imprisoned for treason.

Rather than deny the charges, Hitler admitted he had tried to overthrow the democratic government and outlined his reasons, portraying himself as a true German patriot and the democratic government itself, its founders and leaders, as the real criminals. Newspapers quoted Hitler at length. Thus, for the first time, the German people as a whole had a chance to become acquainted with this man and his thinking. By the time the trial ended, the three presiding judges had become so sympathetic toward Hitler that they agreed to find him guilty only after being assured he would be given an early parole. Thus Hitler received a guilty verdict and a five-year sentence, with eligibility for parole in six months.

PLANNING THE FUTURE

On April 1, 1924, prisoner Adolf Hitler was taken to the old fortress at Landsberg and given a spacious private cell with a fine view. He received gifts, was allowed visitors at will, and had his own private secretary, Rudolph Hess. Hitler used his time in prison to dictate his book *Mein Kampf (My Struggle)* which outlined his political and racial ideas in brutally intricate detail.

Hitler also gave considerable thought to his failed revolution, realizing his attempt to overthrow the government had been foolhardy. He was determined not to repeat that mistake. Although overly eager members of the Nazi Party still clamored for revolutionary action, Hitler now had a better idea. To take over Germany, the Nazis would simply play by the democratic rules and get elected. He confided to a friend:

> Instead of working to achieve power by an armed coup we shall have to hold our noses and enter the Reichstag [Germany's national legislature]. . . . If outvoting them takes longer than outshooting them, at least the results will be guaranteed by their own

During his prison term for his role in the rebellion, Hitler (fourth from right, pictured with his co-conspirators) realized that the Nazis could only come to power through popular election.

Constitution! Any lawful process is slow. But sooner or later we shall have a majority—and after that Germany.[8]

Hitler reorganized the Nazi Party, setting it up like a shadow government, so that when power was achieved this government-in-waiting could slip right into place. Planning for the day when they would rule Germany, the Nazis divided the country into thirty-four districts, or *Gaue*, each one having a *Gauleiter*, or district leader appointed by Hitler and directly responsible to him. The *Gau* itself was subdivided into counties, and each one had a *Kreisleiter*, or county leader who answered to the *Gauleiter*. The counties were subdivided

into local groups. In big cities, those groups were divided along streets and blocks. This kind of meticulous organization allowed Hitler to exert personal control over the entire Nazi hierarchy.

For young people, the *Hitler Jugend*, or Hitler Youth, was established. It was for boys aged fifteen to eighteen, and was modeled after the popular Boy Scout programs. Younger boys age ten to fifteen could join the *Jungvolk*. There was also an organization for girls called *Bund Deutscher Maedel* and for women, the *Frauenschaften*.

Hitler and his Nazi storm troopers, the *Sturmabteilung* or SA, now adopted a brown-shirted outfit, with leather jack boots, swastika armband, badges, and cap. These uniforms, along with the swastika flags, served as important tools in promoting the Nazi Party.

FLEETING SUCCESS

Despite this huge reorganization effort, the Nazis ran into an unexpected obstacle that hindered the party's growth. Things were slowly getting better in Germany. The economy was improving and unemployment had dropped. Factory output was increasing as investment capital poured in from the United States. The Allies had even reduced their demands for war reparations, helping to stabilize the mark. As things improved, a sense of ease set in among the German people, and they saw less reason to favor radical politicians such as Hitler.

Politically, things had also improved, creating another obstacle for Hitler. Germany's democratic government was now led by an esteemed new president, Paul von Hindenburg, a famous World War I field marshal. He was unanimously backed by the conservative and middle-of-the-road political parties, in part to prevent radical parties such as the Nazis from gaining power. As a result, the Nazi Party stagnated, and most attempts by Nazis to get elected to the German Reichstag (legislature) met with mixed results.

However, on October 29, 1929, everything changed. On Wall Street in New York, the stock market crashed. First in America, then across the world, companies went bankrupt, banks failed, and people lost their life savings. Unemployment soared, spreading hunger and homelessness. Governments seemed powerless to halt this worldwide phenomenon. Fear ruled the day. Nations stood on the brink of chaos. Adolf Hitler and his supporters knew their time had come.

Hitler (left) sits with fellow inmates at Landsberg prison. Hitler spent most of his sentence writing Mein Kampf, *a book outlining his brutal political and racial philosophies.*

THE AMAZING SPEAKER

From the very beginning, Hitler's uncanny ability to sense what was on the mind of the average German and speak to the heart of the issue attracted many new followers. Kurt Ludecke, an early supporter, recalls Hitler's oratorical abilities in this excerpt from The Rise to Power: *vol. 1 of* Naziism: A Documentary Reader:

"My critical faculty was swept away. Leaning from the rostrum as if he were trying to impel his inner self into the consciousness of all these thousands, he was holding the masses, and me with them, under an hypnotic spell by the sheer force of his conviction. . . . I do not know how to describe the emotions that swept over me as I heard this man. His words were like a scourge. When he spoke of the disgrace of Germany, I felt ready to spring on any enemy. His appeal to German manhood was like a call to arms; the gospel he preached, a sacred truth. . . . I forgot everything but the man; then glancing around, I saw that his magnetism was holding these thousands as one. Of course I was ripe for this experience. I was a man of thirty-two, weary with disgust and disillusionment, a wanderer seeking a cause, a patriot without a channel for his patriotism, a yearner after the heroic without a hero. The intense will of the man, the passion of his sincerity, seemed to flow from him into me. I experienced an exaltation that could be likened only to religious conversion."

As a gifted public speaker, Hitler was able to appeal to the sentiments of the average German.

GREAT DEPRESSION— GREAT OPPORTUNITY

The worldwide economic collapse of 1929 struck Germany particularly hard. The German economy was especially vulnerable since it was largely sustained by foreign capital, mostly loans from America. When those loans suddenly came due and when the world market for German exports dried up, German industry ground to a halt and workers lost their jobs.

Overnight, the middle class standard of living enjoyed by countless German families evaporated, hurling them into poverty and despair. Making matters worse, Germany's political leaders appeared weak-willed and indecisive, failing to enact desperately needed legislation. Their inaction prompted President Hindenburg to dissolve the Reichstag and schedule new elections for July 1930.

Hitler and his followers seized this golden opportunity to get Nazis elected. Hitler crisscrossed the country by airplane, giving speech after speech promising work to the unemployed; prosperity to failed business people; expansion to the army; social harmony to idealistic students; and restoration of German glory to those in despair. He pledged to make Germany strong again; halt war reparations; tear up the Treaty of Versailles; stamp out corruption; keep down Marxism; and deal harshly with the Jews, whom he continued to use as a scapegoat for Germany's problems.

On election day, September 14, 1930, the Nazis received over 6 million votes, nearly 18 percent of the total, entitling them to 107 seats in the Reichstag. It was a stunning victory for Hitler. Overnight, the Nazi Party went from the smallest to the second largest in Germany.

Buoyed by this big success, Hitler decided to run for the presidency itself in 1931. He received an impressive 30 percent of the vote but lost the election to the incumbent Hindenburg. It was, however, only a minor setback. Time was still on his side as Germany's economic problems steadily worsened, leaving 6 million unemployed. Political stagnation also continued as the Reichstag failed to enact needed legislation.

More and more people began to view the Nazi Party and its dynamic leader as a possible solution to the economic and political mess. When the next election occurred in July 1932, the Nazis received 37 percent of the vote, granting them 230 seats, making them the largest and most powerful group in the Reichstag. This new status emboldened Hitler, and he immediately demanded concessions from President Hindenburg, including office of chancellor for himself. Meanwhile, Nazis in the Reichstag deliberately brought the government of Germany to a complete standstill to exacerbate the crisis and increase the pressure on Hindenburg.

The German people were without jobs, without food, and desperate for relief. Seeing no alternative, President Hindenburg caved in. At noon, on January 30, 1933, a new chapter in German history began as a teary-eyed Adolf Hitler emerged from the presidential palace, bearing the title of chancellor of Germany. Surrounded by admirers, he got into his car and was driven along the street lined with cheering supporters. "We've done it! We've done it!"[9] a jubilant Hitler shouted to them.

2 Bloodless Conquest: Hitler's Gangster Diplomacy

Adolf Hitler, a man who had spent his entire political career denouncing and attempting to destroy Germany's democratic republic was now its principal leader. Upon hearing the news, an old comrade of Hitler's, former army general Erich Ludendorff, became worried. Ludendorff had once supported Hitler and had even participated in the failed Beer Hall Rebellion in 1923, but had since broken off from Hitler. Ludendorff sent a telegram to President Hindenburg with the following warning:

> By appointing Hitler Chancellor of the Reich [German nation] you have handed over our sacred German Fatherland to one of the greatest demagogues [false leaders] of all time. I prophesy to you this evil man will plunge our Reich into the abyss and will inflict immeasurable woe on our nation. Future generations will curse you in your grave for this action.[10]

DEMOCRACY UNDONE

Within weeks of his appointment as chancellor, Ludendorff's warning seemed to come true: Hitler begin to dismantle Germany's democratic government. On the night of February 27, 1933, the Reichstag building, seat of Germany's national legislature, was set ablaze. Although the exact sequence of events is not known, Nazi storm troopers were involved, along with a known arsonist.

Hitler blamed the Reichstag fire on a widespread Communist conspiracy. Although there was little real threat from Communists, Hitler demanded an emergency decree to overcome the supposed crisis. President Hindenburg gave in and signed an emergency law entitled, "The decree for the Protection of the people and the State," which stated:

> Restrictions on personal liberty, on the right of free expression of opinion, including freedom of the press; on the rights of assembly and association; and violations of the privacy of postal, telegraphic and telephonic communications and warrants for house searches, orders for confiscations as well as restrictions on property rights, are permissible beyond the legal limits otherwise prescribed.[11]

Immediately, truckloads of Nazi storm troopers roared through the streets, rounding up accused political opponents by the thousands. They were thrown into hastily constructed holding pens inside old army barracks and abandoned factories. Once inside, the prisoners were subjected to harsh discipline, beatings, and outright torture.

All over Germany, the Nazis began a systematic takeover of government offices. Armed storm troopers would barge into local government buildings, using the emergency decree to throw out legitimate office holders, replacing them with Nazi commissioners. Now, as democracy waned, Hitler demanded the passage of an additional law that would make dictatorship legal. Officially entitled the Law for Removing the Distress of the People and the Reich, this Enabling Act, as it came to be known, granted Hitler extraordinary constitutional powers, including the ability to pass laws, control the budget, and approve treaties with foreign governments. On March 12, 1933, under threat of violence from Nazi storm troopers, politicians in the Reichstag who had once opposed Hitler sided with the Nazis and voted to pass the Enabling Act, bringing democracy in Germany to an end.

FÜHRER OF GERMANY

Although Hitler had acquired the legal authority to function as dictator, one political obstacle still prevented him from wielding absolute power. Hitler was held back by the continued presence of Germany's esteemed eighty-seven-year-old president, Paul von Hindenburg, and his non-Nazi supporters who included many wealthy and powerful Germans along with senior

The Reichstag building (seat of the German legislature) burns in February 1933. Hitler blamed the fire on a Communist conspiracy.

military officials. By mid-1934, however, Hindenburg's health began to decline rapidly.

Hitler quickly made plans to capitalize on the old man's demise. When Hindenburg finally died on August 2, 1934, Hitler immediately abolished the office of president and had himself proclaimed as führer of Germany. To further cement his authority, Hitler required the German Officer Corps and every individual soldier in the German army to swear a brand new oath of allegiance:

I swear by God this sacred oath: I will render unconditional obedience to Adolf Hitler, the führer of the German nation and people, Supreme Commander of the Armed Forces, and will be ready as a brave soldier to risk my life at any time for this oath.[12]

The oath was unprecedented in German history because it was to Hitler personally, not the German state or constitution, as were previous army oaths. Obedience to Hitler would thus be regarded as a sacred duty by all men in uniform, in accordance with their age-old military code of honor, making the German army the personal instrument of the führer.

However, the once-mighty German army was presently in a sorry state, having been stripped bare after World War I in accordance with the Treaty of Versailles. Now, exercising his authority, Hitler set Germany on the path that

The entire contingent of the German Officer Corps swears an oath of allegiance to Hitler in 1934. The oath required the German army to follow Hitler's orders without question.

would ultimately lead to World War II and the death of some 50 million persons: He decided to rearm.

REBUILDING THE ARMY

In flagrant violation of the Treaty of Versailles, Hitler announced in March 1935 that Germany would reintroduce military conscription (compulsory enrollment) and build a new army comprising thirty-six divisions, totaling 550,000 soldiers. This was a direct affront to the European victors of World War I, France and Britain, who had stipulated in the Treaty of Versailles that the German army was not to exceed one hundred thousand soldiers.

Following Hitler's brazen announcement, the whole world waited to see how the leaders of France and Britain would react. Some of Hitler's more cautious army generals even worried France might attack Germany. But nothing happened, except for a few meager diplomatic protests. Hitler, for the first time in his career, had gambled against Germany's former enemies and won. He knew that France was suffering from serious political disunity at the hands of its squabbling politicians. England, with its severe economic troubles, was also weakened. Hitler wagered correctly that the two countries, given their sizable domestic problems, would not respond militarily.

Nevertheless, Hitler decided it would be wise to soothe the jangled nerves of the world's leaders. On May 21, two months after announcing rearmament, he appeared before the Nazi Reichstag in Berlin and delivered a conciliatory speech. "Germany wants peace. . . . None of us means to threaten anybody,"[13] de-

clared Hitler. He then announced an impressive thirteen-point peace program to allay the fears of Germany's neighbors that Germany had any ill intentions. Hitler's method of diplomatic brinkmanship was thus established. A bombastic announcement would usually be followed by a conciliatory speech full of reassuring promises designed to keep world leaders off guard, paving the way for his next venture.

THE FIRST EXPANSION

Hitler's next gamble a year later was one of the biggest risks of his entire career. Beginning at dawn on Saturday, March 7, 1936, three battalions of German soldiers crossed the Rhine River and entered the industrial heartland of Germany known as the Rhineland. This area included all territory west of the Rhine River, extending to the French border, as well as a portion east of the river, including the cities of Cologne, Duesseldorf, and Bonn. The maneuver was yet another gross violation of the Treaty of Versailles since the Allies had designated this area as a nonmilitary or demilitarized zone to safeguard the western European countries Germany had previously attacked, including France.

Despite the hostile move, Hitler appeared before the Nazi Reichstag and gave yet another reassuring speech: "We pledge that now, more than ever, we shall strive for an understanding between European peoples, especially for one with our Western neighbor nations. . . . We have no territorial demands to make in Europe! . . . Germany will never break the peace."[14]

BURNING BOOKS AND IDEAS

Shortly after the Nazis came to power, an event unseen in Europe since the Middle Ages occurred: book burning. Such a scene is described here by Louis P. Lochner, then head of the Associated Press Bureau in Berlin, reprinted from Nazism: A Documentary Reader. *vol. 1* State, Economy and Society:

"The whole civilized world was shocked when on the evening of May 10, 1933 the books of authors displeasing to the Nazis, including even those of our own [American author] Helen Keller, were solemnly burned on the immense [plaza] between the University of Berlin and the State Opera [House] on Unter den Linden. I was a witness to the scene. All afternoon Nazi raiding parties had gone into public and private libraries, throwing onto the streets such books as Dr. Goebbels [Hitler's propaganda minister] in his supreme wisdom had decided were unfit for Nazi Germany. From the streets, Nazi columns of beer-hall fighters had picked up these discarded volumes and taken them to the square above referred to. Here the heap grew higher and higher, and every few minutes another howling mob arrived, adding more books to the impressive pyre. Then, as night fell, students from the university, mobilized by the little doctor, performed veritable Indian dances and incantations as the flames began to soar skyward. When the orgy was at its height, a cavalcade of cars drove into sight. It was the Propaganda Minister himself, accompanied by his bodyguard and a number of fellow torchbearers of the new Nazi *Kultur* [way of life]. 'Fellow students, German men and women!' he cried as he stepped before a microphone for all Germany to hear him. 'The age of extreme Jewish intellectualism has now ended, and the success of the German revolution has again given the right of way to the German spirit. . . . You are doing the right thing in committing the evil spirit of the past to the flames at this late hour of the night. It is a strong, great and symbolic act, an act that is to bear witness before all the world to the fact that the spiritual foundation of the November Republic [post–World War I democracy] has disappeared. From these ashes there will arise the phoenix of a new spirit. . . . The past is lying in flames. The future will rise from the flames within our own hearts. . . . Brightened by these flames our vow shall be: The Reich and the Nation and our führer Adolf Hitler: Heil! Heil! Heil!'"

Once again, the whole world waited to see how the French and British would react. German troops entering the Rhineland had orders to scoot back into Germany if the French army attacked. But in France, the politicians were unable to convince their reluctant generals to act, and were unable to get any British support for a military response. So they did nothing. The French army, one hundred divisions strong, never budged against the thirty thousand lightly armed German soldiers occupying the Rhineland, even though France and Britain were both obligated by the Treaty of Versailles to preserve this demilitarized zone.

It had been a tremendous gamble for Hitler, one that might have cost him everything if his troops had been humiliated by their old enemies. Later, Hitler privately admitted:

> The forty-eight hours after the march into the Rhineland were the most nerve-racking in my life. If the French had then marched into the Rhineland we would have had to withdraw with our tail between our legs, for the military resources at our disposal would have been wholly inadequate for even a moderate resistance.[15]

Hitler's troops had carried the swastika banner into the Rhineland and received a heroic welcome. They were met by priests conferring blessings and women tossing flowers. In Cologne, the people were delirious with joy. Inside Cologne's Roman Catholic cathedral, Cardinal Schulte praised Hitler for sending the army, thus restoring German military control over the Rhineland, which Germans there had long desired. Throughout Germany, the bold and daring leader, Adolf Hitler, rose to new heights of popularity.

PLANNING FOR WAR

In his public utterances, Hitler was very careful to reassure nervous Europeans that Germany's military buildup was solely a defensive measure designed to put the country on an equal footing with its neighbors. In private, however, Hitler told a very different story. In November 1937 he assembled Germany's highest ranking military leaders and bluntly announced he intended to launch a large-scale war of conquest in Europe as soon as the German military was ready to strike. After swearing his generals to secrecy, Hitler told them:

> The history of all ages—the Roman Empire and the British Empire—had proved that expansion could only be carried out by breaking down resistance and taking risks. . . . The question for Germany was: Where could she achieve the greatest gain at the lowest cost?[16]

Hitler outlined various scenarios in which the first objective would be the seizure of neighboring Austria and Czechoslovakia to protect Germany's eastern and southern flanks. Depending on the degree of political instability in France, Hitler explained, the new war might begin in 1938 or as late as 1943 when Germany would be fully rearmed.

Hitler's casual acceptance of the immense risks of starting a new war in Europe shocked his generals. They especially urged him not to provoke Britain and

GERMAN PREWAR EXPANSION

(map labels)

SWEDEN
LATVIA
LITHUANIA
Baltic Sea
Polish Corridor
GREAT BRITAIN
EAST PRUSSIA
GERMANY
Danzig
THE NETHERLANDS
RHINELAND 1936
○ Berlin
BELGIUM
POLAND
LUXEMBOURG
RHINELAND
SUDETENLAND
BOHEMIA & MORAVIA
CZECHOSLOVAKIA 1939
SAAR
CZECHOSLOVAKIA
SLOVAKIA (To Hungary 1939)
FRANCE
SUDETENLAND 1938
SWITZERLAND
AUSTRIA
HUNGARY
ROMANIA
AUSTRIA 1938
ITALY
YUGOSLAVIA
Adriatic Sea
Mediterranean Sea
U.S.S.R.

Germany 1933
Areas Annexed 1936–1939

France. To Hitler, their reluctance revealed they lacked the degree of nerve and boldness he desired. After the meeting, he decided to shake up his military staff by ousting his top generals and a host of senior generals, replacing them with younger men eager to serve him and follow his orders, regardless of the consequences.

In addition, Hitler restructured the entire military command, giving himself supreme authority over the German army, navy, and air force. Thus, by the beginning of 1938, the people of Germany, along with their entire armed forces, had come under the control of one man, the führer, Adolf Hitler.

THE FALL OF AUSTRIA

Only nineteen months would elapse from the moment Hitler secured control of the German armed forces until the actual start of World War II. During those months, as Germany rearmed and prepared for war, Hitler engaged in a kind of gangster diplomacy by which he repeatedly bullied, threatened, bluffed, and lied to various European leaders in order to expand Germany's borders without firing a shot.

The first target was neighboring Austria, a German-speaking country. Austria was already being torn apart by Nazi sympathizers working day and night to undermine the Austrian government and pave the way for Hitler. Hoping to save his country from the looming disaster, Austria's leader, Dr. Kurt von Schuschnigg, traveled to Hitler's mountain retreat at Berchtesgaden for a face-to-face meeting.

At that meeting, the quiet-spoken Austrian chancellor was lambasted without mercy by Hitler. "You have done everything to avoid a friendly policy!"[17] Hitler yelled, telling him that Austria was isolated and could not count on France or England to halt a Nazi invasion. A string of threats by Hitler was followed by the presentation of a document containing a list of demands granting Nazis in Austria sweeping powers, including control of the police. In addition, Nazis were to be appointed as minister of war, and minister of finance, with preparations made for the assimilation of Austria's entire economy by Nazi Germany.

The Austrian chancellor hesitated to sign such a shocking document, whereupon Hitler told him, "You will either sign it as it is and fulfill my demands within three days, or I will order the march into Austria."[18] The Austrian chancellor returned home to contemplate Hitler's demands and to discuss them with the country's president. Meanwhile, Hitler ordered General Wilhelm Keitel to conduct army maneuvers near the Austrian border to make it appear an invasion was imminent. The bluff worked. The Austrians granted most of Hitler's demands, including control of the police. As a result, emboldened Nazi agitators roamed the streets, tearing down the Austrian flag and raising the swastika

German soldiers roll into Prague in March 1939. Czechoslovakia was the first non-German speaking territory to be conquered by the Nazis.

banner as police stood by and watched.

In a desperate last-minute bid to halt the collapse of his country and to stave off Hitler, Chancellor Schuschnigg scheduled a national election to allow the Austrians to vote on whether their country should remain independent from Nazi Germany. Hitler, on hearing of this act of blatant defiance by Schuschnigg, flew into a rage and decided to send in the German army.

Chancellor Schuschnigg, aware of the pending invasion, canceled the election and even resigned his post to appease Hitler. But it was to no avail. At dawn on Saturday, March 12, 1938, German soldiers in tanks and armored vehicles roared across the German-Austrian border. They met no resistance and in most places were welcomed like heroes. Many of Austria's 7 million ethnic Germans longed to attach themselves to the rising star of Germany and its dynamic führer.

When news of the invasion reached Britain and France, leaders there reacted just as they had when Hitler occupied the Rhineland a few years earlier: They did nothing. In France, internal political problems once again prevented any military response. Britain, now led by Prime Minister Neville Chamberlain, was fully committed to preserving peace. Making matters worse, Austria, proud and defiant in its hour of need, never formally requested any outside assistance.

Following the *Anschluss* (forced union) of Austria with Nazi Germany, the people of Czechoslovakia next door were confronted with the reality that they were now surrounded on three sides by Hitler's army. Hoping to soothe their fears and keep them off guard, Hermann Göring, Hitler's second in command, as-

sured the nervous Czech government, "I give you my word of honor that Czechoslovakia has nothing to fear from the Reich."[19]

HITLER APPEASED

The little democratic republic of Czechoslovakia, created by the Western Allies after World War I, had been hampered from day one by serious ethnic conflict among its diverse peoples. The young country was home to Czechs, Slovaks, Hungarians, and over 3 million ethnic Germans living in the western part of the country known as the Sudetenland. Like the Austrian Germans, they longed to attach themselves to Hitler's Germany.

To open the door for Hitler, Nazi agitators in the Sudetenland utilized the same tactics that Austrian Nazis had used so successfully. Throughout the summer of 1938, they provoked political and social disturbances to destabilize their government. Responding to this carefully orchestrated crisis, Hitler and Göring publicly stated the German army might need to enter the Sudetenland to restore order.

Czechoslovakia, allied with Britain and France, depended upon these nations for its security. With Germany edging toward military action against Czechoslovakia, British prime minister Neville Chamberlain requested a face-to-face meeting with Hitler. The sixty-nine-year-old Chamberlain arrived at Hitler's Berchtesgaden villa on the morning of September 15, 1938. At the same location six months earlier, Austria's chancellor had tried to negotiate with Hitler but had been relentlessly badgered. This time, in

Hitler meets with British prime minister Neville Chamberlain in September 1938 to discuss the annexation of the Sudetenland, a region of Czechoslovakia where millions of Germans lived.

addressing the head of government of the British Empire, Hitler avoided such crude tactics. However, he politely asked Chamberlain if the Sudetenland, with its sizable German population, could simply be handed over to Nazi Germany.

Chamberlain, devoted to peace, said he needed to consult with his cabinet in London and asked Hitler to delay military action until he returned for his next visit. Hitler agreed to the delay. Chamberlain then returned to London and obtained his government's approval for the Sudetenland concession. He also received a favorable response from the leaders of France. The Czechs themselves had little say and were mostly left out of the discussions.

Chamberlain returned to Germany on September 22 and told Hitler he could annex the Sudetenland. "I am terribly sorry," Hitler responded, "but . . . this plan is no longer of any use."[20] Hitler now demanded a full German army occupation of the Sudetenland and the expulsion of all non-Germans living there. Chamberlain, utterly flabbergasted, informed Hitler this amounted to an ultimatum and returned to London deeply upset.

The French, on hearing of Hitler's demands, mobilized one hundred army divisions and began positioning troops along the French-German border. The Czech army, consisting of a million men, was also mobilized. Britain put its entire naval fleet on alert and declared a state of emergency in London.

With Europe now gearing up to oppose him, Hitler decided to give diplomacy one last chance. He sent a letter to Chamberlain promising that if the west-

---

LIFE IN HITLER'S GERMANY

Dr. George Wittenstein is one of only two survivors of the inner circle of the White Rose, a resistance group of anti-Nazi college students and their supporters that openly opposed Hitler. In 1997 he gave a fascinating lecture to a Jewish organization in Los Angeles from which this excerpt is taken:

"It is my firm belief that no one raised in the United States can fully comprehend what it is like to live under an absolute dictatorship. . . . The government—or rather, the [Nazi] Party—controlled everything: the news media, arms, police, the armed forces, the judiciary system, communications, travel, all levels of education from kindergarten to universities, all cultural and religious institutions. Political indoctrination started at a very early age, and continued by means of the Hitler Youth with the ultimate goal of complete mind control. Children were exhorted in school to denounce even their own parents for derogatory remarks about Hitler or Nazi ideology. My own teenage cousin, for instance, threatened to denounce his father; and I was barely able to deter him by pointing out to him that he himself might end up destitute if his father were arrested and incarcerated. Organized resistance was practically impossible. One could not speak openly, even with close friends, never knowing whether they might not be Nazi spies or collaborators. So well organized was the control and surveillance by the Party, that each city block had a Party functionary assigned to spy on his neighbors. This *Blockwart* was ostensibly responsible for the well being of the residents of his city block, but in reality had to monitor, record and report on activities, conversations, and remarks of each person, as well as on their associations. Even the privacy of one's home was not assured: a tea cozy [placemat] or pillows placed over the telephone were popular precautions against eavesdropping by bugging. Nor did one ever know what mail had been secretly opened. I remember only too well an incident in a cinema: someone sitting a few rows in front of me was led away by the Gestapo [secret police]. Apparently he had made a derogatory remark to his companion about Hitler during the preceding newsreel. Whoever had overheard him must have, as a patriotic duty, tipped off the secret police."

ern Allies allowed the German army to occupy the Sudetenland, Germany would join with England and France in guaranteeing the rest of Czechoslovakia from aggression. Chamberlain grasped this last chance for peace and agreed to attend a joint summit in Munich, Germany, that would include himself, Hitler, and the leaders of France and Italy. Just after 1 A.M. on September 30, 1938, the four leaders signed the Munich Agreement allowing Hitler to acquire the Sudetenland via a military occupation and to expel the non-Germans.

Upon arriving back in London, a greatly relieved Chamberlain declared, "The settlement of the Czechoslovakian problem, which has now been achieved, is, in my view, only the prelude to a larger settlement in which all Europe may find peace."[21] For Hitler, however, the Munich Agreement was a worthless piece of paper. Just three weeks after signing the document, he instructed his generals to make plans to seize the remainder of Czechoslovakia.

CZECHOSLOVAKIA DISAPPEARS

Using the same tactics that had worked so well before, the Nazis encouraged political unrest in what remained of Czechoslovakia to serve as an excuse for military action. Hitler convinced the Slovaks in eastern Czechoslovakia to break off and form their own country, which they did. Following this, all that remained of Czechoslovakia were the two central provinces of Bohemia and Moravia.

Hoping to stave off the complete collapse of his country, Czechoslova-

kia's President, Emil Hácha, asked Hitler for a face-to-face meeting. When the two men met in Berlin, Hitler bullied Hácha without mercy, making accusations of alleged wrongs committed by Czechs against ethnic Germans in Czechoslovakia. Hitler then informed Hácha his patience had ended and said the German army was about to invade his country. The Czech people, Hitler declared, had just two options: They could resist the invasion and be violently crushed or peacefully receive the incoming troops.

A document, tantamount to surrender, was then presented to the Czech president, but he refused to sign. Hitler's second in command, Hermann Goering, then threatened to have Prague, the Czech capital and a beautiful historic city, blasted to ruins by the German air force. Upon hearing this, the frail president fainted. When he revived, the Nazis stuck a telephone in his hands, connecting him with his government back in Prague. Hácha spoke into the phone and reluctantly advised his government to surrender peacefully to the Nazis. He then signed the document, stating he had "confidently placed the fate of the Czech people and country in the hands of the führer of the German Reich."[22]

Two hours later, amid a late winter snowstorm, the German army rolled into the first non–German speaking territory to be taken by the Nazis. In justifying the invasion, Hitler declared, "Czechoslovakia showed its inherent inability to survive and has therefore now fallen victim to actual dissolution."[23] Meanwhile, the whole world waited to see how Prime Minister Chamberlain would react.

Prime Minster Chamberlain holds a copy of the Munich Agreement, a treaty whose terms Hitler ignored when he invaded Czechoslovakia.

BRITAIN DRAWS THE LINE

At first, Chamberlain responded to Hitler's aggression by claiming the British were not bound to protect Czechoslovakia since the country in effect no longer existed after the Slovaks had broken off to form their own country. The prime minister's feeble response caused an uproar in the British press and in the House of Commons, where angry members vowed that England would never again appease Hitler.

Following this, Chamberlain had a change of heart. In a speech, broadcast on radio throughout England, Chamberlain apologized for his initial reaction to Hitler's actions in Czechoslovakia. Then he announced Britain was drawing the line:

> [Hitler] has taken the law into his own hands. . . . Is this the last attack upon a small state or is it to be followed by others? Is this, in effect, a step in the direction of an attempt to dominate the world by force? . . . No greater mistake could be made than to suppose that because it believes war to be a senseless and cruel thing, this nation has so lost its fiber that it will not take part to the utmost of its power in resisting such a challenge if it ever were made.[24]

Now, for the first time, the British were standing up to Hitler, indicating they were willing to fight. British diplomats officially informed the Nazis that Hitler's occupation of Czechoslovakia was "a complete repudiation of the Munich Agreement . . . devoid of any basis of legality."[25] The French also stated they would not recognize the legality of the German occupation.

On March 31, 1939, in an ominous development for Hitler, Britain and France both went beyond mere diplomatic protests. Prime Minister Chamberlain issued a solid declaration, with the backing of France, guaranteeing Germany's northern neighbor, Poland, from Nazi aggression. Hitler brushed it aside and, unfazed by the British and French, at least for the time being, ordered his generals to begin planning for the invasion of Poland.

Chapter

3 Blitzkrieg: The Lightning War

Thus far, all of Hitler's conquests had resulted from his successful use of gangster diplomacy. But in mid-1939, for the first time in his career, Hitler encountered an opponent that would not give in. For months, Hitler had been pressuring the leaders of Poland to give him the former German city of Danzig and to allow construction of a new highway and railroad from Germany through Polish territory into East Prussia.

The territory in question was known as the Polish Corridor, a narrow strip of land which gave Poland access to the sea and cut off East Prussia from the rest of Germany. Poland had been granted this sea corridor after World War I by the Treaty of Versailles, which also designated Danzig, located on the Baltic Sea, as a Free City, belonging to no country, but administered by Poland. All of this was unacceptable to Hitler, and to most Germans, but they had never had the power to do anything about it—until now.

Despite increasing pressure from Hitler, the Poles stood their ground and bluntly informed the Nazis that any attempt to seize Danzig would inevitably lead to conflict. Prime Minister Chamberlain also warned Hitler that Britain, with the backing of France, would fight to save Poland from the Nazis.

LAST-MINUTE ALLIANCE

Hitler was undeterred by Chamberlain's warning. As Germany's army geared up for battle, the major powers in Europe and elsewhere began to choose sides in case of war. Britain and France were already allied with Poland. The United States, most diplomats assumed, would side with Britain at some point. Germany's main friend in Europe, Fascist Italy, led by the dictator Benito Mussolini, announced its military alliance with Hitler.

For the time being, Soviet Russia remained neutral, until Russian foreign minister Vyacheslav Molotov gave a speech in the spring of 1939 suggesting to the western Allies that they should begin negotiations soon or there might be some kind of agreement forthcoming between Russia and Nazi Germany.

However, Prime Minister Chamberlain, leader of the western Allies, had little faith in the ability of Russia's army and thus saw no value in a British-Soviet military alliance. Britain, along with Poland, therefore refused all Soviet offers to discuss joint military action in the event of further Nazi aggression. This rejection encouraged Josef Stalin, leader of Soviet Russia, to negotiate with Hitler.

Soviet leader Josef Stalin (second from right) looks on as Soviet and Nazi representatives sign the Non-Agression Pact in 1939.

Hitler was eager to deal with Stalin. The time line for Hitler's master war plan involved crushing Poland, beginning in September 1939, then quickly turning his troops westward to attack France. Hitler needed a peace agreement with Russia to forestall the possibility of a two-front war, with Germany sandwiched in the middle, fighting the French and British in the west and the Russians in the east.

In August, Nazi foreign minister Joachim von Ribbentrop went to Moscow to seal an agreement. In a ceremony at the Kremlin, attended by Stalin himself, Ribbentrop signed the Nazi-Soviet Non-Aggression Pact. As a result, Hitler would not have to fight a war on two fronts. Stalin, for his part, was granted a free hand in eastern Europe, pending the outbreak of war, to annex several areas lost to Russia at the end of World War I, including the countries of Latvia, Estonia, and Finland, and, most importantly, the entire eastern portion of Poland.

News of the surprise pact shocked the world. The Nazi-Soviet alliance effectively sealed the fate of Poland, a country geographically isolated from its western allies, making direct military aid nearly impossible. With the Soviets now cooperating and Hitler determined to seize more territory, a new war in Europe seemed all but certain.

THE EVE OF WAR

The ink on the Non-Aggression Pact was barely dry when Hitler assembled his top generals at his Berchtesgaden villa and gave them the green light to invade Poland. He explained, "Our economic situation is such that we cannot hold out more than a few years. . . . We have no other choice. We must act."[26] Thus far, all of Germany's territorial gains had resulted from political bluffs, but this time it would be necessary to rely on German military might. Setting the tone for the coming conflict, he told the generals how they should behave:

> I shall give a propagandist [contrived] reason for starting the war. Never mind whether it is plausible or not. The victor will not be asked afterward whether he told the truth or not. In starting and waging a war it is not right that matters but victory. . . . Close your hearts to pity! Act brutally! Eighty million people must obtain what is their right. . . . The stronger man is right. . . . Be harsh and remorseless! Be steeled against all signs of compassion![27]

By nightfall on Thursday, August 31, 1939, 1.5 million German soldiers were moving into position along the Polish border. To justify the planned invasion, the Nazis staged fake attacks against German troops near the Polish border, making it appear they were under siege. At the same time, a Polish-speaking German, working with the Nazis, broadcast an inflammatory speech in Polish over the radio, saying, "People of Poland, the time has come for war between Poland and Germany!"[28] This gave Hitler the excuse he needed.

LIGHTNING WARFARE BEGINS

The German people had surrendered their will to one man, Adolf Hitler, and he now plunged them into a new war in Europe. At dawn on Friday, September 1, 1939, German troops roared into Poland via several gigantic mechanized formations, smashing all opposition in sight. It was the first time the world had ever witnessed what became known as blitzkrieg (lightning warfare) involving highly coordinated attacks of planes, tanks, motorized artillery, and troops.

The outgunned Polish army, comprising thirty-five divisions, totaling half a million soldiers, fought bravely against this mechanized onslaught. But with their airfields and warplanes demolished by air attacks in the early hours of the invasion, and lacking sufficient firepower, Polish defensives were split apart, then surrounded and destroyed. In just a few days, the entire Polish army was on the verge of annihilation as the Germans relentlessly pressed their advantage. German tank commander, General Erwin Rommel, commented on the blitzkrieg phenomenon:

> Against a motorized and armored enemy, non-motorized infantry divisions are of value only in prepared

positions. Once such positions have been pierced or outflanked and they are forced to retreat from them, they become helpless victims of the motorized enemy.[29]

Motorized columns of German infantry roared through the countryside at speeds up to forty miles per hour heading for Poland's major cities. By September 6, Kraków, Poland's second most important city, had fallen. At Warsaw, the country's capital, the government fled into exile, signaling the end of organized resistance. The Germans quickly overtook the remnants of the Polish army. It had taken just eighteen days for Poland to be conquered by Hitler's incredible military machine.

With victory in Poland secured, Hitler ordered his troops westward to the German-French border to prepare for the next phase of war. Meanwhile, the Russians took the opportunity to fulfill their portion of the Nazi-Soviet Pact and invaded Poland from the east, taking nearly half of Poland.

Nazi soldiers advance through a bombed-out Polish town in 1939. The Nazis overwhelmed the Polish army in a matter of days.

THE BRITISH AND FRENCH REACT

Just hours after the invasion of Poland had commenced on September 1, British and French diplomats in Berlin presented a formal demand that Hitler's troops in Poland halt their aggression and prepare to withdraw. To Hitler, this request was ludicrous, and he ignored it. Two days later, early Sunday morning, September 3, the British delivered an ultimatum declaring that a state of war would exist by 11 A.M. that day unless a positive response was received to their original demand for a cessation of hostilities. Just after the 11 A.M. deadline passed, the Nazis announced they flatly refused to cooperate. Following the British example, the French presented their own ultimatum which also received a negative response.

French soldiers keep watch at a fort on the Maginot Line along the border with Germany. French soldiers waited tensely at the border for months as the Nazis prepared to invade France.

Blaring loudspeakers in Berlin then made it official, informing the people they were at war. Germans everywhere reacted to the announcement with stunned silence. Although they supported Hitler, they did not favor war, having lost millions of countrymen two decades earlier during World War I, the bloodiest conflict up to that time. The people of Britain and France reacted the same way. There were no cheering crowds or marching bands as there had been at the outbreak of World War I.

Hitler, a decorated veteran of World War I, tried to reassure the German people, telling them, "I am from now on just the first soldier of the German Reich. I have once more put on that [World War I style] coat that was most sacred and dear to me. I will not take it off again until vic-tory is secured, or I will not survive the outcome."[30]

Despite their declarations of war, the French and British, beset by internal political strife and guided by cautious generals who had witnessed the horrific carnage of World War I, hesitated to take immediate action. This resulted in a prolonged standoff.

THE PHONY WAR

With the German army still preoccupied in Poland, the French had a huge advantage on Germany's western border. A hundred French divisions stood ready for attack, while Hitler had just twenty-three divisions to hold them back, until reinforcements could arrive from Poland.

At this point, a French attack into western Germany might have halted further Nazi aggression by disabling Germany's vital war industry in the Ruhr Valley. However, the French, who had suffered more during World War I than any other nation, yielded to caution. French generals chose a defensive posture, relying on a series of newly built steel and concrete fortifications known as the Maginot Line to ward off Hitler. Four divisions of British soldiers joined the French and also stood by on the defensive.

Unlike his foes, Hitler was not one to hesitate. Buoyed by the amazing speed of his victory in Poland and reacting to the timidity of the French and British, Hitler assembled his top generals on September 27, 1939, and ordered them to prepare for an attack against France.

After giving this order, Hitler resumed his old habits and once again portrayed himself in public as a man of peace. During a speech on October 6, he questioned the need for conflict in western Europe, offering a vaguely worded peace proposal to Britain and France and requested a conference of European leaders.

However, the leaders of Britain and France, having been fooled once by Hitler, flatly turned him down. Reacting to their rejection, the Nazis claimed Hitler's generous peace offer had been spurned, and that if war erupted in western Europe, the blame would lie with Britain and France.

Preparing for the coming battle, Hitler's generals rushed reinforcements to western Germany until the number of German troops roughly equaled the number of French and British troops positioned in eastern France. However, when all the troops were finally assembled, strangely, nothing happened. Instead of charging into battle as Hitler wanted, his generals, mindful of Germany's strategic errors in World War I, asked him to delay the attack so they could develop a better battle plan.

As a result, months passed with tens of thousands of troops on both sides staring at each other with hardly a shot fired. The prolonged standoff assumed a somewhat comical aspect, jokingly referred to as the *sitzkrieg* (sit-down war) by the Germans and the "phony war" by the British. For Hitler, however, there was to be nothing phony about the coming fight. As his generals finalized their battle plans, Hitler told them their objective was "the destruction of the power and ability of the Western Powers ever again to be able to oppose the state consolidation and further development of the German people in Europe."[31] Hitler's new date for the invasion of France was May 10, 1940.

PREEMPTIVE STRIKES

Prior to the attack on France, Hitler's generals decided to launch preemptive strikes against Germany's northern neighbors, Norway and Denmark, to secure submarine sea bases and to protect the vital flow of Norwegian iron ore used in German war production.

Beginning on April 9, 1940, a daring seaborne assault was launched by five divisions of German troops against Copenhagen, the Danish capital, and Oslo, the Norwegian capital, along with three Norwegian seaports. In Denmark, as German troops streamed into the country by sea

In 1940 the German navy lands troops at Narvik, Norway, an important seaport. The sea assaults on Norway were met with fierce resistance, but the Nazis ultimately prevailed.

and by land, Germany's ambassador there simply informed the Danish king that his country was now under Hitler's control and that resistance was futile. With his small army overpowered, the king and his government surrendered.

In Norway the Germans had a harder time. The sea assault at Oslo failed due to heavy cannon attacks from ships and coastal fortifications, but German paratroopers managed to capture the city. Norway's king and his government fled into the mountains and implored fellow Norwegians to resist. To aid the besieged Norwegians, the British landed troops at the seaports of Narvik and Trondheim but were unable to hold the cities. As Norway succumbed to the Germans, the British made a hasty exit along with Norway's king who went into exile in London.

BLITZKRIEG RESUMES

With the preemptive strikes completed, the long-awaited attack on France commenced. The battle began with the invasion of France's neutral northern neighbors, Belgium and Holland. This was a deliberate ploy by Hitler's generals to bluff the French and British into believing the main German offensive would be coming through Belgium, just as it had during World War I.

Meanwhile, the main blow against France came four days later through the Ardennes Forest toward the south. Utilizing the same style of blitzkrieg that had worked so well in Poland, German tanks and motorized infantry ripped through the lightly defended forest, then roared northward through France to trap French

and British armies that had fallen for the bluff and moved into Belgium.

By May 20, just ten days after the invasion began, six British divisions and three entire French armies were cut off in Belgium with their backs to the sea. The Germans then tightened the noose, squeezing the French and British into a small pocket around the seaport of Dunkirk. At this point, however, one of the stranger twists of World War II occurred as Hitler's armored units unexpectedly halted their advance. *Luftwaffe* chief Hermann Göring, seeking to impress Hitler, had boasted that his air force alone could destroy the troops. Josef Schmid, a *Luftwaffe* intelligence officer, remembered:

> Goering described the situation at Dunkirk in such a way as to suggest there was no alternative but to destroy by an attack from the air . . . and pointed out that the advance elements of the German army, already battle weary, could hardly expect to succeed in preventing the British withdrawal. He even requested that the German tanks, which had reached the outskirts of the city, be withdrawn a few miles in order to leave the field free for the *Luftwaffe*. Hitler . . . agreed to the proposal.[32]

The British seized this opportunity to begin a mass evacuation from Dunkirk. The Royal Navy, aided by small merchant ships, fishing boats, and pleasure crafts of all sizes, worked around the clock. British soldiers lined up along the beach, waiting for rescue. As one officer remembered, "Our only thoughts now were to get on a boat. Along the entire queue not a word was spoken. The men just stood there silently staring into the darkness, praying that a boat would soon appear, and fearing that it would not."[33]

Over nine days, amid constant air attacks from Göring's planes, some three hundred thousand soldiers were ferried to safety across the English Channel, including sixty thousand Frenchmen. Most of the soldiers left their weaponry behind, escaping only with the clothes on their back. The remaining troops were not so lucky. German armored columns finally rolled into Dunkirk on June 4, taking thousands of French prisoners. The German army then turned itself around and sped away to crush what was left of France's army elsewhere.

THE FRENCH CRUMBLE

The French army, demoralized by indecisive generals, was on the verge of collapse. A French observer recalled spending an hour with army commander General Georges Blanchard inside his headquarters: "During all that time, he sat in tragic immobility, saying nothing, doing nothing, but just gazing at the map spread on the table between us, as though hoping to find on it the decision which he was incapable of [making]."[34]

The Germans, with twice as many available troops and ten armored divisions in the field, overwhelmed France's remaining troops. On June 10 the French government fled Paris, declaring it an un-

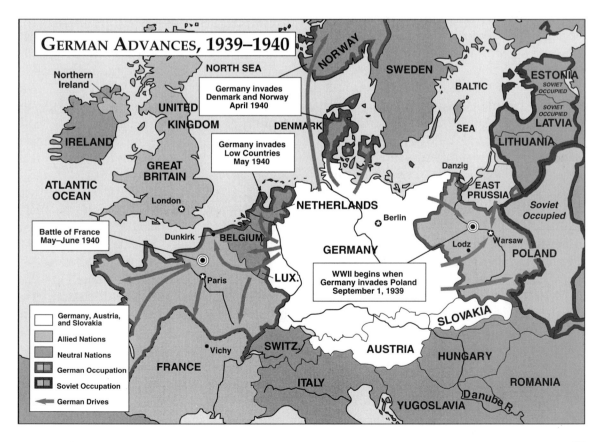

defended city. Four days later, German troops raced in and immediately hoisted the swastika flag on the Eiffel Tower, the symbol of France. On June 17 the French asked for surrender terms.

The conquest of France by the earth-shattering blitzkrieg had taken just six weeks. Wallowing in the magnitude of this spectacular victory, Hitler personally accepted the surrender of France inside the identical railroad car, and on the exact spot, where Germany had surrendered to France two decades earlier, ending World War I.

Surrender terms required the French to hand over all anti-Nazi refugees along with the entire French naval fleet. To encourage French cooperation, Hitler left southern France unoccupied and allowed day-to-day administration of the whole country to remain in French hands. A collaborationist regime, headed by prestigious French marshal Henri Pétain of World War I fame, was granted the authority to run France, but remained subordinate to Hitler.

Nine European countries, Austria, Czechoslovakia, Poland, Norway, Denmark, Belgium, Luxembourg, Holland, and France, had fallen under Hitler's control since 1938, either through political coercion or brute military force. Other European countries had forged alliances with Hitler, including Spain and Italy. Only one major European power, Britain, remained to challenge Hitler's new empire.

Britain Carries on Alone

Britain now had a new prime minister named Winston Churchill, a gifted orator and impassioned anti-Nazi who had been denouncing Hitler for years. Upon the collapse of France, Churchill implored his people to keep fighting:

> Hitler knows that he will have to break us . . . or lose the war. If we can stand up to him all Europe may be free, and the life of the world will move forward into broad, sunlit uplands; but if we fail, then the whole world, including the United States, and all that we have known and cared for, will sink into the abyss of a new dark age. . . . Let us therefore brace ourselves to our duties and so bear ourselves that, if the British Empire and its Commonwealth last for a thousand years, men will say: "This was their finest hour."[35]

Hitler had never met Churchill and assumed the new prime minister, like his predecessor Chamberlain, could be toyed with through negotiations. To tempt Churchill into negotiating, Hitler made an offer he considered generous. He would leave Great Britain and its colonies around the world untouched if the British would adopt a hands-off policy and allow Nazi domination of Europe. But Churchill flatly refused all of Hitler's attempts to negotiate.

Thus far, during Hitler's reign of power, every European leader he challenged had either backed down or been conquered. Enraged by Churchill's blatant defiance, Hitler ordered his generals to invade the British Isles. Code-named Operation Sea Lion, the battle plan they concocted involved a ground invasion by German troops ferried across the English Channel from France. However, from the beginning there were doubts the plan would succeed. Britain was defended by an immensely powerful navy that could blast any seaborne troops out of the water. In addition,

Britain's Fiery New Leader

Upon first entering the British House of Commons as prime minister in May 1940, Winston Churchill received only a lukewarm reception from the assembly, while at his side, outgoing prime minister Neville Chamberlain was heartily cheered. Churchill then made a brief statement, which became one of the greatest calls to arms ever uttered, as noted in Churchill: A Biography *by Roy Jenkins:*

"I would say to the House, as I said to those who have joined this government, that I have nothing to offer but blood, toil, tears and sweat. We have before us an ordeal of the most grievous kind. . . . You ask, what is our policy? I will say: It is to wage war, by sea, land and air, with all our might and with all the strength that God can give us: to wage war against a monstrous tyranny, never surpassed in the dark, lamentable catalogue of human crime. That is our policy. You ask, what is our aim? I can answer in one word: It is victory, victory at all costs, victory in spite of all terror, victory, however long and hard the road may be; for without victory, there is no survival."

When Winston Churchill became Britain's prime minister in 1940, he urged the entire country to unite to defeat the Nazis.

---

the British could hurl dozens of home-based army divisions against German troops trying to come ashore. Realizing the difficulties a land invasion would pose, Hitler chose an unprecedented alternative—wage war from the sky.

The Battle of Britain

Germany's air force chief, Hermann Göring, had boasted to Hitler that his warplanes alone, without the help of the German army or navy, could force a British surrender. Hitler took his word for it. On August 15, 1940, the Battle of Britain began, involving an air attack against the British by the world's largest air force.

The initial plan was to wipe out Britain's air defense, the Royal Air Force (RAF), by destroying its airfields, warplane factories, and radar posts. Scurrying aloft to challenge this aerial onslaught were dazzling new British Spitfire and Hurricane fighter planes. For three solid weeks, the German and British planes battled furiously. German planes attacked by the hundreds, but the speedy British fighters, guided by newly developed radar, were more nimble than the German fighters. Richard Hillary, a British pilot, recalled his feelings toward the German in his gun sight: "I wondered what he was like, this man I would kill. Was he young, was he fat, would he die with the führer's name on his lips, or would he die alone. . . . I would never know."[36]

Day by day, losses for both sides mounted. The RAF shot down over a thousand German planes, but the British were running desperately low on fighters and were flying their last reserves. The Germans stood on the brink of victory by sheer weight of numbers, with hundreds more aircraft than the British. But the Germans were unaware the RAF was nearly defeated. Remarkably, in one of the major turning points in World War II, the Germans suddenly shifted their attacks away from the battered RAF facilities and airfields. Instead, they began launching nightly terror bombings against the people of London to force a quick surrender.

THE BLITZ

Beginning on September 7, 1940, and for a total of fifty-seven consecutive nights, London was bombed. Each night, as the air raid sirens shrieked, the people scurried into subway stations and basements for shelter, listening to the thunderous rain of destruction falling from the sky. Crowded together on makeshift beds, some slept, while others stayed nervously awake all night. In the morning

Smoke rises above London during the air raids known as the Blitz. For fifty-seven nights in 1940, the Germans bombed London in an effort to force a British surrender.

King George VI and Queen Elizabeth inspect Buckingham Palace after a night of heavy German bombing. The palace was one of several landmarks damaged during the Blitz.

they emerged to observe the wreckage of their homes and shops and to see the ruins of cherished historical buildings.

Hitler's intention was to break the morale of the British people so they would pressure Churchill into negotiating with him. However, the bombings, known as the Blitz among the British, had the opposite effect. Encouraged by Churchill's frequent public appearances and inspiring radio speeches, the British pulled together, determined to hold out.

In retaliation for the Blitz, British bombers raided Berlin (Nazi Germany's capital) and Munich. Although the initial bombings were limited in scope, they came as a shock to the German people, who had been assured their cities were impenetrable. An infuriated Hitler responded to the air raids by adding a dozen British cities to the target list including Birmingham, Liverpool, and historic Coventry, which was leveled. In London, on the night of December 29, 1940, the Germans dropped incendiary bombs that created a firestorm devastat-

ing the area around St. Paul's Cathedral. Other damaged landmarks in London included Buckingham Palace, Westminster Abbey, and the House of Commons. By the end of 1940, the Britist death toll had surpassed fifteen thousand.

Despite the carnage, the Blitz was failing to achieve its objective. With the Germans focusing their attacks exclusively on Britain's cities, the wounded RAF was able to rebuild its damaged airfields, train new pilots, and repair aircraft. As a result, RAF fighters in increasing numbers shot down the incoming bombers. The Germans began losing skilled pilots and bomber planes by the hundreds, with no end in sight.

Realizing his air force was unable to conquer Britain, Hitler called off the Blitz and all plans for the invasion of England. Instead, he ordered the *Luftwaffe* to transfer its entire resources to eastern Europe. Nazi Germany, Hitler had decided, could quickly end the war and achieve final victory, not by conquering Britain, but by conquering Russia.

4 Quest for Lebensraum: The Fateful Attack on Russia

The first volume of Adolf Hitler's book *Mein Kampf* described his fundamental belief that Germany's survival depended on its ability to acquire vast tracts of lebensraum (living space) in eastern Europe, including Russia. This new land would be used to cultivate food and provide room for the expanding German population at the expense of the people already living there who were to be removed, enslaved, or killed.

According to Hitler, such drastic actions were justified purely on racial grounds. In *Mein Kampf*, Hitler explained his racial thinking. He categorized people based on physical appearance alone, thus establishing higher and lower orders of humans. The supreme human form, according to Hitler, was the person of Aryan origin, characterized by his or her fair skin, blond hair, and blue eyes. Hitler considered all other humans to be racially inferior, particularly the Jews and the Slavic peoples of eastern Europe, including the Russians. Nazi racial philosophy, as Hitler explained in *Mein Kampf*, "by no means believes in an equality of races . . . and feels itself obligated to promote the victory of the better and stronger, and demand the subordination of the inferior and weaker."[37]

Acting on that belief, Hitler had launched a war of conquest in Europe. Now, in the spring of 1941, as absolute ruler of much of western Europe and in supreme control of the world's most powerful army, Hitler decided to launch an attack in the east against Russia to acquire the lebensraum he felt Germany deserved, despite the fact he had signed a non-aggression pact with the Russians.

AN ORDER TO KILL

For Hitler, the coming attack in the east would be unlike anything ever seen. In contrast to the military tactics used to conquer Germany's western neighbors, in the east the objective was to wage a war of total annihilation. In March 1941 Hitler gathered his top generals and told them how their troops should behave:

> This struggle is one of [political] ideologies and racial differences and will have to be conducted with unprecedented, unmerciful and unrelenting harshness. All officers will have to rid themselves of obsolete [moral] ideologies. . . . I insist absolutely that my orders be executed without contradiction. The commissars [Russian leaders] are the bearers of ideologies

directly opposed to National Socialism. Therefore the commissars will be liquidated. German soldiers guilty of breaking international law . . . will be excused [that is, not held responsible for their actions].[38]

This command, known as the Commissar Order, ordered the killing of all persons with political authority in Russia. Hitler considered communism, the political system the commissars ran in Russia, directly opposed to Nazism, since it had been founded by Karl Marx, who was Jewish. Thus he denounced everyone affiliated with the Russian political system.

For Hitler's generals, the Commissar Order posed a dilemma. On the one hand, they felt obligated to follow Hitler's orders, no matter how extreme, since they had all sworn an oath of obedience to the führer. However, they also felt obligated to follow traditional codes of military conduct, considered obsolete by Hitler, which prohibited the murder of civilians. In the end, however, despite their misgivings, not one of the generals opposed Hitler's order. Instead, they dutifully set about the task of planning the invasion of Russia, knowing the attack would unleash an unprecedented wave of murder.

OPERATION BARBAROSSA

The battle plan for the conquest of Russia was named Operation Barbarosa (Red Beard) by Hitler to honor Frederick I, nicknamed Red Beard, a medieval warrior

Nazi soldiers execute Ukranian Jews at a mass grave. To carry out such actions, Hitler instructed his generals to abandon traditional codes of military conduct.

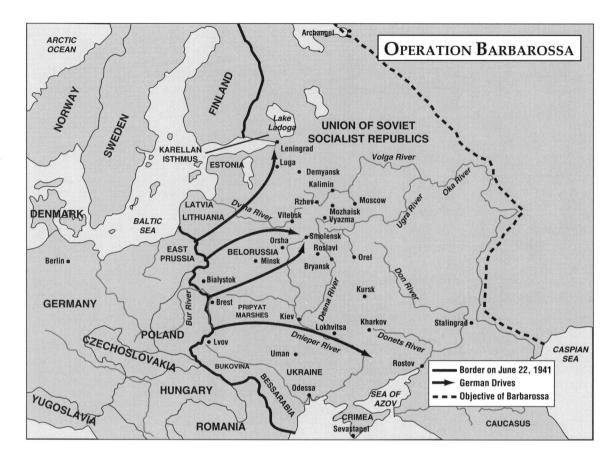

Border on June 22, 1941
German Drives
Objective of Barbarossa

who had ruled Germany and surrounding areas. The plan called for blitzkrieg on a continental scale. Three army groups, involving 160 divisions, were to attack on May 15, 1941. Their goal was to reach the Volga River deep in the heart of Russia and achieve victory by the end of summer.

Hitler and his command staff believed the Russian army, which they estimated at two hundred divisions, would not be effective as a fighting force and would fall apart, just as the Polish army had in 1939, but on a much larger scale. Their belief was based in part on Nazi racial thinking: Since the Russians were a Slavic people, Hitler and his generals were convinced they were inferior and

could not defend themselves against an army of racially superior Germans.

As the May 15 launch date for the invasion neared, however, a series of unexpected problems arose that upset Hitler's carefully laid plans. Hitler's friend and chief ally in Europe, Benito Mussolini, the leader of Italy, trying to imitate Hitler's brash style, had launched a surprise attack against Greece. British troops in the Mediterranean then rushed in to help the Greeks fend off the Italians.

The arrival of British troops in southern Europe meant major trouble for Hitler. Their presence threatened Germany's southern flank, making it necessary for Hitler to secure this region of Europe, known as the Balkans, before launching his invasion of Russia. To help secure the area, Hitler forged an alliance with two Balkan countries, Bulgaria and Yugoslavia.

In Yugoslavia, however, no sooner had the government allied with Hitler than it was overthrown by its own citizens. On hearing the news, Hitler flew into a rage and ordered his generals to conquer the country at once. As a result, beginning on April 6, 1941, the German army roared into Yugoslavia and Greece, taking both countries and expelling the British. The German army also occupied neighboring Romania, Bulgaria, and Hungary, thus securing the Balkans. However, these military actions delayed the invasion of Russia for five weeks, a time element that would have crucial consequences.

THE INVASION BEGINS

At 3:30 a.m., on Sunday, June 22, 1941, Operation Barbarossa finally commenced as 3 million German soldiers plunged headlong into Russia. To the German people, Adolf Hitler announced, "I have decided again today to place the fate and future of the Reich and our people in the hands of our soldiers. May God aid us, especially in this fight."[39]

Astoundingly, up to this point, Russia's leader, Josef Stalin, had unwisely disregarded a flurry of intelligence reports that a Nazi invasion was pending. As a result, Russian troops in the path of the invading Germans were taken by surprise. As the Germans approached, Russian field commanders made frantic calls to headquarters asking for orders, but were told there were no orders. Sleepy-eyed Russian soldiers scrambled out of their tents, only to find themselves already surrounded by German troops, with no option but to surrender. Numerous important bridges were captured undamaged, and hundreds of Russian planes sitting on the ground were destroyed.

The multi pronged German blitzkrieg surged forward day after day across a thousand-mile front, conquering whole armies of hapless Russians. Georgy Semenyak, then a twenty-year-old soldier, remembered:

> It was a dismal picture. During the day airplanes continuously dropped bombs on the retreating soldier. . . . When the order was given for the retreat, there were huge numbers of people heading in every direction. . . . The lieutenants, captains, second-lieutenants took rides on passing vehicles . . . mostly trucks traveling eastwards. . . . And without commanders, our ability to defend ourselves was so severely weakened that there was really nothing we could do.[40]

Two weeks into the invasion, most observers, including Hitler and his command staff, believed they were about to trounce the Russians and snatch another quick victory. German forces, operating in three gigantic army groups, proceeded like clockwork toward their destinations. Army Group North, with six armored divisions and twenty-one infantry divisions, headed for Leningrad (now St. Petersburg) located on the Baltic Sea. This city of palaces and fine old buildings had once served as Russia's capital and had been built by Czar Peter the Great in the 1700s.

As German troops neared the city, Hitler ordered it flattened. Regarding the people of Leningrad, Hitler told his generals, "The problem of the survival of the population and of supplying it with food is one which cannot and should not be solved by us. In this war for existence we have no interest in keeping even a great part of the city's population."[41]

Meanwhile, Army Group Center, the largest of the three groups, with thirty infantry and fifteen motorized divisions, continued on its seven-hundred-mile-long journey toward Russia's capital, Moscow. At the same time, Army Group South, with five panzer tank divisions and twenty-five infantry divisions, headed for Kiev, capital of Ukraine, considered the breadbasket of Europe with its fertile wheat fields.

THE RUSSIANS RESIST

For Hitler and his command staff, all that remained was for the Russians to concede defeat and accept their fate. But much to Hitler's surprise, the Russians kept on fighting. Despite staggering losses of soldiers and equipment, and against overwhelming odds, pockets of unexpected resistance emerged that battled furiously, unlike anything the Germans had encountered. These Russians were determined to fight to the death, unlike their comrades who had easily surrendered when the invasion began.

Complicating matters for Hitler, his generals had grossly underestimated the total strength of the Russian army. Instead of two hundred divisions, the Germans encountered nearly four hundred. Although hundreds of thousands were cap-

tured or killed, thousands more soldiers appeared to take their place. In addition, these replacements were supported by T-34 tanks with armor plating so thick it caused German antitank shells to ricochet harmlessly. The Germans had no idea the Russians had produced such a powerful tank. The capacity of Russian war production, in addition to Russian troop strength, had obviously been misjudged. Not only could the Russians produce a tank superior to anything in the German arsenal at that time, but they also churned out state-of-the-art warplanes in enormous numbers to bomb and strafe frontline German troops.

Making matters worse for the Germans, Russian army generals, who were in chaos when the invasion began, had regained their composure. They formed strong defensive lines in the path of the advancing Germans. The stiffening resistance, combined with mounting logistical problems including overextended supply lines, slowed the progress of Hitler's three army groups. By August 1941 it had become apparent to the German high command there would be no speedy victory in Russia. "The whole situation makes it increasingly plain that we have underestimated the Russian colossus,"[42] commented General Halder, a top aide to Hitler. A vital strategic question then arose over whether to follow the original battle plan or make changes to adapt.

Army Group Center was now about two hundred miles from Moscow, poised for a massive assault on the Russian capital. However, the original battle plan called for Army Groups North and South to conduct the main attacks in Russia, with Army Group Center relegated to a supporting role. A majority of Hitler's se-

Soviet T-34 tanks move into position to resist the invading Germans. The technologically advanced T-34 completely took the Germans by surprise.

nior generals now advised scrapping the original plan in favor of an all-out offensive against Moscow. If the Russian capital fell, they argued, it would be a devastating blow to Russian morale, knock out the country's main transportation hub, and drastically reduce Russian war production. Russia's days would then be numbered, they asserted. The final decision, however, rested solely with the supreme commander, Adolf Hitler.

A MOMENTOUS DECISION

In what was perhaps his single most important decision during World War II, Hitler decided to pass up the chance to capture Moscow during the summer of

1941. Instead, he stayed with the original plan to crush Leningrad in the north and seize Ukraine in the south. This, Hitler told his generals, would be far more devastating to the Russians than the fall of Moscow. A successful attack in the north would wreck the city named after one of the founders of communism, Vladimir Lenin. Attacking the south would cause the destruction of formidable Russian armies protecting the region and would place vital agricultural and industrial areas in German hands.

Although they disagreed with the orders of their supreme commander, the German generals dutifully halted their advance on Moscow and moved troops away from Army Group Center to aid Army Groups North and South. By late

September, bolstered by additional panzer tanks and infantry divisions, Army Group South successfully seized the city of Kiev in Ukraine, capturing over six hundred thousand Russian soldiers, according to German estimates.

Now, with most of Ukraine conquered, and Leningrad surrounded, the generals implored Hitler to let them focus on the capture of Moscow before the onset of winter. But Hitler denied their request and instead ordered a simultaneous attack involving all three army groups, stretching their resources to the limit.

ATTACK ON MOSCOW

All eyes were on the calendar as the long-delayed push toward Moscow finally began. It was now October 2, and there was a noticeable chill in the morning air. In some places, snowflakes already wafted from the sky. The notoriously severe Russian winter was just around the corner.

At first, it appeared Moscow might fall. Two Russian armies defending the outer approach to the city were encircled by Germans who took another six hundred thousand prisoners, according to

Nazi soldiers retreat after failing to take Moscow. The staunch resistance of Russian troops and the onset of a brutal winter thwarted Hitler's 1941 advance into the Soviet Union.

An Uncaring Commander

As supreme commander of the German army, Hitler spent much time studying maps and ordering large-scale military maneuvers with little regard for the soldiers involved, as German field marshal Erich von Manstein commented, reprinted from The Third Reich: A New History *by Michael Burleigh:*

"He was a man who saw fighting only in terms of the utmost brutality. His way of thinking conformed more to a mental picture of masses of the enemy bleeding to death before our lines than to the conception of a subtle fencer who knows how to make an occasional step backwards in order to lunge for the decisive thrust. For the art of war he substituted a brutal force which, as he saw it, was guaranteed maximum effectiveness by the willpower behind it. . . . Despite the pains Hitler took to stress his own former status as a front-line soldier, I still never had the feeling that his heart belonged to the fighting troops. Losses, as far as he was concerned, were merely figures which reduced fighting power. They are unlikely to have seriously disturbed him as a human being."

German estimates. By October 20, units of the German army had advanced to within forty miles of Moscow. The Soviet government, including Stalin himself, prepared to evacuate.

To Hitler, it seemed his lifelong dream of conquering the East and acquiring lebensraum was going to be achieved. Confident of victory, Hitler broadcast a radio message to the German people: "I declare today, and I declare it without any reservation, that the enemy in the East has been struck down and will never rise again. . . . Behind our troops already lies a territory twice the size of the German Reich when I came to power in 1933."[43]

But then the weather turned. It began with days of unending rain, a regular part of autumn in Russia. Fields of deep, sticky mud materialized, immobilizing anything on wheels. German armored units lost their tactical maneuverability. The nonstop rain also created miserable conditions for foot soldiers, soaking them to the bone in mud up to their knees. After four months of warfare in Russia, many of these soldiers were already exhausted. In November things worsened when autumn rains abruptly gave way to heavy snowfall. Accompanied by subzero temperatures and frigid winds, soldiers were stricken with a host of cold-related ailments.

The German army had expected a summertime victory in Russia and was totally unprepared for winter warfare. Heavy boots and overcoats, warm blankets, and thick socks desperately needed by suffering field troops were nowhere to be found. German medical officer Heinrich Haape

No Easy Victory

The German military, from Hitler down to the common foot soldier, expected to quickly win the war in Russia, but were sadly mistaken. Fyodor Sverdlov, a company commander in the Soviet 19th Rifle Brigade, remembered how the Germans looked after the failed battle of Moscow (excerpted from War of the Century: When Hitler Fought Stalin *by Laurence Rees):*

"The German Army near Moscow was a very miserable sight. I remember very well the Germans in July 1941. They were confident, strong, tall guys. They marched ahead with their sleeves rolled up and carrying their machine guns. But later on they became miserable, crooked, snotty guys wrapped in woolen kerchiefs stolen from old women in villages. . . . Of course, they were still firing and defending themselves, but they weren't the Germans we knew earlier in 1941."

The Nazis suffered tremendous casualties during the siege of Moscow, shattering the myth of their invincibility.

recalled, "The cold relentlessly crept into our bodies, our blood, our brains. Even the sun seemed to radiate a steely cold and at night the blood red skies above the burning villages merely hinted a mockery of warmth."[44]

Thousands of frostbitten, malnourished frontline foot soldiers dropped out of their units. Motorized troops were plagued by mechanical failures, as tank and truck engines cracked from the cold while iced-up artillery and machine guns jammed. The once mighty German military machine now ground to a halt in Russia.

Russian Revenge

Despite the weakness of his troops, Hitler still believed Moscow could be taken and ordered all available forces in the region to make one final thrust for victory. Beginning on December 1, 1941, German tank formations attacked from the north and south of the city while infantrymen attacked from the east. But the Russians were ready and waiting. The weather delays had given the Russians time to bring in reinforcements, including units specially trained for winter warfare. Wherever the Germans attacked they encountered furious resistance. They were also stricken by temperatures that had now plunged to forty degrees below zero Fahrenheit.

Hitler had pushed his troops beyond endurance, and they now paid a terrible price. Beginning on December 6 a hundred Russian divisions counterattacked the Germans all along the two-hundred–mile front around Moscow. For the first time in the war, the Germans experienced blitzkrieg in reverse, as overwhelming numbers of Russian tanks, planes, and artillery tore them apart. The impact was devastating. By mid-December, German forces around Moscow, battered, cold, and tremendously fatigued, were in full retreat and facing the possibility of being overrun by the Russians.

In the bloodied fields of snow around Moscow, Nazi Germany had suffered its first-ever defeat. The illusion of invincibility that had shaken the world since September 1939 had been broken. By now, a quarter of all German troops fighting in Russia, some 750,000 soldiers, were dead, wounded, missing, or ill.

Reacting to the catastrophe that he had caused, Hitler blamed his military staff, firing dozens of his most experienced field commanders. He then assumed personal day-to-day operational command of the army and promptly ordered all remaining troops in Russia to halt in their tracks and retreat no farther, which they did. All across Russia, the front gradually stabilized. They would hold the lines and wait for spring, when new offensives would bring the victory Hitler felt was sure to come, despite everything.

Although the Russians and British remained to be beaten, Hitler could still gaze at a map that showed a Nazi empire stretching from the outskirts of Moscow all the way to Paris, and from Norway into the north to Greece. Indeed, inside this empire, a reign of terror was now underway comprising one of the most savage episodes in human history.

5 Absolute Power—Absolute Terror

Battles and occupations were one aspect of the European experience during World War II. Yet another uniquely horrific chapter, the Holocaust, existed during this time period. The Holocaust was the systematic murder of approximately 6 million Jews by the Nazi regime and its collaborators. Although Jews were the primary victims of the Holocaust, several other groups were also decimated. Gypsies, the handicapped, Poles, Russians, Communists, Socialists, Jehovah's Witnesses, and homosexuals were all deemed racially or physically inferior to Nazis, and so were rounded up and sent to the state-sponsored murder factories known as concentration camps.

The devastation of the Holocaust was staggering. By 1941, when the Nazis began operating concentration camps across Europe, about 1 million Jews perished. By 1945, close to two of every three European Jews had been killed as part of what was known as the "Final Solution," a systematic effort by the Nazis to eradicate the Jewish population.

Throughout the 1930s, Jews had been increasingly persecuted under the Nazi regime. Laws were passed requiring them to wear badges identifying themselves as Jews; these were followed by laws that prohibited them from holding jobs in cer-

tain sectors, owning property, or being present in public places. It was not until the fall of 1938, however, that an outright program of violence against them began.

On the night of November 9, 1938, all over Germany, Jewish shops and synagogues were looted and burned during a Nazi-organized national riot. Private homes were also raided in what became known as *Kristallnacht* or the Night of Broken Glass. At 6 A.M. on November 10, a fourteen-year-old Jewish boy, asleep his family's Berlin apartment, was awakened when the doorbell rang. Years later, he recalled:

I heard the shrill, barking, yelling voices of men. It seemed to me there were at least twenty. . . . "Where are the Jews? Where are they?" they yelled. I heard noises of falling furniture and breaking glass. I could not imagine what was happening. I stood behind my bed when one Nazi in full uniform entered the room. He stepped back a fraction of a second when he saw me. . . . A smell of bad alcohol came out of his mouth. He took another glaring look at me and began to destroy everything within reach. . . . While he was breaking the closet door my mother came into the room. He commanded her to hold the clothes for him so that he would be able to tear them better. . . . We watched the men destroy the whole apartment of five rooms. All the things my parents had worked for eighteen long years were destroyed in less than ten minutes. . . . The Nazis left us yelling, "Don't try to leave this house! We'll soon be back again and take you to a concentration camp to be shot."[45]

GERMAN ANTI-SEMITISM

Although Jews made up less than 1 percent of Germany's prewar population of 55 million, to Hitler and his followers they were considered the mortal enemy of the German people. In his book *Mein Kampf*, Hitler claimed that Jews in Germany and around the world were engaged in an international conspiracy to keep the blond-haired, blue-eyed German master race from assuming its rightful position as rulers of the world. During his rise to power, Hitler also blamed the Jews for the economic, social, and political chaos that plagued Germany in the years after World War I.

The notions of an international Jewish conspiracy and Jewish blame for Germany's various misfortunes became widespread beliefs in Nazi Germany and were taught as facts to impressionable school children. In addition, the Nazi Propaganda Ministry, under the direction of Joseph Goebbels, churned out a ceaseless stream of anti-Jewish leaflets, posters, newspapers, newsreels, speeches, and

A Jewish synagogue in Berlin burns after being set ablaze on November 9, 1938, during the raids on Jewish property known as Kristallnacht.

radio pronouncements. Slowly but surely, Germans of all ages began to turn against the Jews as this incident involving German children illustrates, documented by the Bavarian police:

There were anti-Jewish demonstrations in the swimming pool in Heigenbrueken. Approximately 15–20 young bathers had demanded the removal of the Jews from the swimming bath by chanting in the park which adjoins the bath. . . . A considerable number of other bathers joined in the chanting so that probably the majority of visitors were demanding the removal of the Jews. . . . In view of this incident, the Spa Association today placed a notice at the entrance to the baths with the inscription: 'Entry Forbidden to Jews.'[46]

Over four hundred regulations were eventually issued against Jews in Nazi Germany, prohibiting everything from performing in a symphony orchestra to owning a pet cat. Jewish children were tossed out of the public school system while their parents were banned from most professions. German Jews were also stripped of their citizenship by the Nuremberg Laws which designated them as mere subjects of Nazi Germany and prohibited them from marrying other Germans. As Nazi Germany's borders expanded in 1938 and thereafter, the menace spread. Throughout Europe and Russia, wherever the German army advanced, instruments of Nazi terror known as the Gestapo (secret police) and SS (an abbreviation of Schutzstaffel, Hitler's personal security service) followed. Their task was to subjugate conquered peoples by violently suppressing all resistance. After the people in a newly acquired area were cowed into a state of fearful obedience, their labor could be exploited, along with their industrial and agricultural resources, to serve Nazi Germany.

AUSTRIAN JEWS TARGETED

In such fashions, the Nazis occupied Austria in 1938. The occupation was accompanied by a severe outbreak of anti-Jewish violence. Austria's capital city, Vienna, home to about 180,000 Jews, became the scene of Nazi-organized riots. Police under Nazi control stood by as Jews throughout the city were beaten and humiliated while their homes, businesses, and synagogues were ransacked. Jewish men were grabbed at random and forced to scrub sidewalks and gutters while crowds laughed and jeered. Jews were also forced to clean toilets and the latrines in SS barracks using sacred Hebrew prayer cloths. Walter Kammerling, who was a young Jew in Vienna, remembered, "You sometimes heard screams behind you and you knew people were being beaten up, and you couldn't even turn around. I mean, if you turned around then you were involved. . . . You tried to make yourself invisible."[47]

The beginning of Hitler's war of conquest in 1939 placed whole new populations of Jews under Nazi control. Eastern Europe was home to millions of Jews and other persons considered unwanted by the Nazis such as Gypsies, Communists, and homosexuals. To deal with them, Hitler dispatched his SS fanatics with orders to kill.

NIGHTMARE IN POLAND

Poland, populated by a Slavic people deemed wholly inferior by the Nazis, was destined to become a virtual slave state. Hitler decreed that every facet of Polish culture was to be extinguished. Education was to be abolished so the Poles would degenerate into a population of ignorant, obedient laborers. A memorandum by SS Chief Heinrich Himmler in May 1940 stated:

> The non-German population of the eastern territories must not receive any education higher than that of an elementary school with four grades. The objective of this elementary school must simply be to teach simple arithmetic up to 500 at the most, how to write one's name, and to teach that it is God's commandment to be obedient to the Germans and to be honest, hard working, and well-behaved. I consider it unnecessary to teach reading.[48]

On Hitler's expressed order, all well-educated or influential Poles were to be assassinated by special SS action squads known as *Einsatzgruppen*. Trailing behind the German army, they rounded up and shot thousands of Polish political leaders and intellectuals. Simply wearing a pair of eyeglasses was enough to get one shot,

Pictured are members of an Einsatzgruppe, *one of many elite corps of SS soldiers organized to assassinate Polish leaders and intellectuals.*

since it implied a person was educated.

The SS in Poland also adopted a policy, set by Himmler, of seizing blond-haired, blue-eyed Polish children and shipping them back to Germany to be raised as Nazis. Each year, all children between the ages of six and ten were examined, as Himmler put it "to sort out those with valuable blood and those with worthless blood."[49] Those considered worthless were condemned to a life of forced labor, or worse, if they happened to be Jewish.

Poland was home to about 3 million Jews, the largest population in Europe. To

Stripped of their clothing, Jewish women and children in Ukraine are rounded up for execution. Einsatzgruppen *began to systematically exterminate Jews in the East in 1941.*

cope with what the Nazis described as their "Jewish problem," Himmler's assistant Reinhard Heydrich came up with the idea of herding the Jews into specially established ghettos in Poland at places such as Lodz, Kraków, and Warsaw. The ghettos functioned as huge walled-in prisons, with the Jews cut off from the outside world. A young girl confined inside the Lodz ghetto wrote in her diary, "When we look at the fence separating us from the rest of the world, our souls, like birds in a cage, yearn to be free. . . . How I envy the birds that fly to freedom."[50] At Warsaw, the Nazis squeezed over four hundred thousand Jews into an area that normally held a third of that number, deliberately creating conditions that allowed malnutrition and disease to flourish, killing tens of thousands.

Beginning in June 1941, millions more Jews came under Nazi control as Hitler's armies roared across Russia. For Hitler, the existence of so many of these unwanted people was cause for lethal action.

MASS MURDER BEGINS

Based on the success of the SS *Einsatzgruppen* in Poland, four new groups containing three thousand men were assembled to follow the German army into Russia. Their initial task was to shoot all Communist officials, in accordance with Hitler's Commissar Order. Beginning in August 1941, on orders from Himmler, *Einsatz* units also began shooting Russian Jews wherever they were found. This marked the start of a systematic, coordinated effort by the Nazis to exterminate Jews in the East, rather than relocate them to ghettos.

Throughout Russia, there were thousands of isolated little villages called shtetls populated exclusively by Jews. Arriving in a Jewish village, an SS officer would inform the town's leading citizens the entire population was about to be resettled. Instead, they were transported to an isolated area just outside the town.

Otto Ohlendorf, an *Einsatz* group chief, explained what happened next:

> They were ordered to hand over their valuables to the leader of the unit, and shortly before their execution to surrender their outer clothing. The men, women and children were led to a place of execution which in most cases was located next to a deeply excavated anti-tank ditch. Then they were shot, kneeling or standing, and the corpses thrown into the ditch.[51]

As German troops advanced deeper into Russia and Ukraine, they encountered ever-increasing numbers of Jews. With tireless devotion, *Einsatz* units rounded up and murdered these Jews. Group commanders even competed to tally the highest overall death numbers and sent detailed reports back to Himmler. One of the largest massacres occurred over two days in September 1941 when 33,771 Jews in Ukraine were rounded up and taken to the Babi Yar ravine outside Kiev. One of the few survivors, Dina Pronicheva, remembers:

> It was dark already. . . . They lined us up on a ledge which was so small that we couldn't get much of a footing on it. They began shooting us. I shut my eyes, clenched my fists, tensed all my muscles and took a plunge down before the bullets hit me. It seemed I was flying forever. But I landed safely on the bodies. After a while, when the shooting stopped, I heard the Germans climbing into the ravine. They started finishing off all those who were not dead yet, those who were moaning, hiccuping, tossing, writhing in agony. . . . They started covering the corpses over with earth. They must have put quite a lot over me because I felt I was beginning to suffocate. . . . Then I decided it was better to be shot than buried alive. Using my left arm I managed to move a little way up. Then I took a deep breath, summoned up my waning strength and crawled out from under the cover of earth . . .

The Nazis began using mobile gas vans like this one to exterminate Jews in the East after deciding that gas was a more humane form of execution than shooting.

was lucky enough to crawl up one of the high walls of the ravine, and straining every nerve and muscle, got out of it.[52]

Curious about the extermination process, Himmler decided to watch an *Einsatz* firing squad execute a hundred Jews in Russia. This administrator of mass murder had, ironically, never seen a man killed. An SS man who was present later recalled that Himmler seemed on the verge of fainting as the firing squad blasted away. When a second set of Jews went before the same firing squad, the shots failed to kill two women. A highly emotional Himmler shouted for them to be put out of their misery. As a result of this experience, Himmler ordered Jewish women and children to be killed in newly developed mobile gas vans whenever possible, a method he considered more humane for the victims and less traumatic for his SS executioners.

These vans marked the beginning of Nazi efforts to employ deadly gas to exterminate Jews rather than roving firing squads. Each gas van contained an airtight rear compartment into which the engine's exhaust fumes were fed while the van was driven toward a mass grave. The vans, however, presented their own set of problems. The amount of time it took for people to perish varied widely, causing some to arrive at the grave site still alive. Removal of the bodies from the rear of the van had also become a ghastly task for the SS men involved.

Although the vans were troublesome, the idea of gassing Jews took hold. At Himmler's request, SS officials began experiments utilizing airtight chambers in concentration camps. Exhaust fumes were piped into the chambers, each about the size of a large room, from an engine mounted just outside. Additional experiments involved the use of disinfectant pellets known as Zyklon-B, which gave off deadly cyanide fumes when exposed to air.

While the gassing experiments were underway, mass shootings of Jews continued all over occupied Russia with the death tally eventually surpassing a million. For the Nazis, however, the question still remained of what to do with the millions of Jews under their control elsewhere in Europe.

THE FINAL SOLUTION

By 1941 Hitler had decided to exterminate the entire Jewish population of Europe and Russia and had selected his loyal SS to fulfill this mission. To coordinate the task, Reinhard Heydrich convened the Wannsee Conference in Berlin, attended by fifteen high-ranking Nazi bureaucrats, and told them, "Europe will be combed [of Jews] from west to east."[53] Statistics at the time indicated there were 11 million Jews in Europe. The initial goal, as Heydrich explained, was to deport the Jews to the ghettos of Poland and concentration camps where they would be allowed to perish through a combination of hard labor and deprivation. Jews who survived this ordeal would be finished off in the gas chambers.

In the summer of 1941 Himmler summoned an SS officer named Rudolf Hoess to Berlin for a meeting. Hoess, who had trained at the concentration camp Dachau, was the commandant of a

CONCENTRATION CAMPS THROUGHOUT EUROPE

LATVIA

Baltic Sea

LITHUANIA

Neuengamme

Bergen-Belsen

NETHERLANDS

Sachsenhausen-Oranienburg

Ravensbrück

EAST PRUSSIA

Stutthof

POLAND

GERMANY

Treblinka

Chelmno

Gross-Rosen

Sobibor

Majdanek

Mittelbaudora

Auschwitz-Birkenau

Belzec

BELGIUM

Flossenbürg

Theresienstadt

CZECHOSLOVAKIA

Zweiler-Struthof

Mauthausen

FRANCE

Dachau

HUNGARY

ROMANIA

SWITZERLAND

AUSTRIA

- Detention camps/Gestapo prisons
- ◐ Large-scale labor camps
- ▢ Large-scale extermination camps

ITALY

YUGOSLAVIA

Adriatic Sea

BULGARIA

Mediterranean Sea

newly established concentration camp in the town of Oswiecim, Poland, which the Nazis called Auschwitz. At the meeting, Himmler informed Hoess, "The führer has ordered the Final Solution of the Jewish question. We, the SS, have to carry out this order. . . . I have therefore chosen Auschwitz for this purpose."[54]

At Auschwitz, a gigantic new annex was constructed called Birkenau, containing four large gas chamber–crematory buildings and scores of huts for slave laborers. From the moment it became operational, Birkenau served as the focal point of the Nazi effort to exterminate the Jews. Seven days a week, around the clock, trainloads of Jews arrived from all over Europe. They were immediately subjected to a hasty life-and-death selection process. Children, the elderly, and anyone deemed unfit for slave labor were ushered away to an undressing room adjacent to the gas chamber. They were given a piece of soap and taken into what appeared to be a large shower room, but which was actually a gas chamber. The door was then slammed shut and the lights turned off. From above, an SS man poured pellets of *Zyklon-B* into hollow floor-to-ceiling shafts made of perforated sheet metal, giving off cyanide fumes that oozed out at floor level and then rose up toward the ceiling. Children died first since they were closer to the floor. Pandemonium usually erupted in the chamber as the bitter almondlike odor of the gas seeped higher, with adults climbing on top of each other, forming a tangled heap of dead bodies all the way up to the ceiling.

Auschwitz was not the only camp to employ gas chambers. Other highly efficient killing facilities also located in occupied Poland included Belzec, Treblinka, and Sobibor, along with Majdanek and Chelmno.

At each of the death camps, special squads of Jewish slave laborers called *Sonderkommandos* untangled corpses and removed them from the gas chambers. They extracted gold fillings from teeth and searched the bodies for hidden valuables. The corpses were disposed of by various methods including mass burials and cremation in open fire pits or in specially designed crematory ovens. All clothing, money, gold, jewelry, watches, eyeglasses, and other valuables were sorted out, and then shipped back to Germany. Women's hair was sent to a firm in Bavaria for the manufacture of felt.

Those who were deemed strong and/or healthy were, for the time being, spared the gas chambers but were put to grueling work. Concentration camp inmates labored from morning till night, subjected to frequent beatings by overseers, while subsisting on starvation rations of watered-down soup and an ounce of bread. Up to eight hundred people were crammed into each barrack without any privacy or adequate sanitation. Alice Lok, who survived Auschwitz, recalled, "Six people slept on a plank of wood . . . and if one had to turn, all the others had to turn because it was so narrow. One cover, no pillow, no mattress."[55] Inmates unable to work for any reason were sent straight to the gas chambers.

EUROPE ENSLAVED

In addition to the mass murder of Jews, Hitler's SS routinely rounded up non-Jews throughout occupied Europe to serve as slave laborers in German factories and farms or in hundreds of specially built Nazi work camps. With most of Germany's able-bodied men serving in the armed forces, and Hitler forbidding the use of German women as laborers, the Nazis faced a desperate labor shortage, requiring millions of foreign workers.

Drastic measures used by the SS in occupied territories included cordoning off a few city blocks or a whole town and seizing every able-bodied person within that area, then shipping them in boxcars to Germany. A young Ukrainian woman recalled, "They went from house to house and took away all of the young people. They took us to a big school and at five o'clock in the morning to the station. There they shoved us into railway wagons which were then bolted. The journey

THE ORDEAL OF AUSCHWITZ

Jews arrived around the clock at Auschwitz and were immediately subjected to a life-and-death selection process. Eighteen-year-old Alexander Ehrmann and his family arrived from Hungary in the spring of 1944 and were confronted by the notorious SS Dr. Josef Mengele, as recalled in Auschwitz: 1270 to the Present *by Deborah Dwork and Robert Jan van Pelt:*

"We arrived around one o'clock in the morning in an area with lights, floodlights, and stench. We saw flames, tall chimneys. We still did not want to accept that it was Auschwitz. . . . The train stopped. Outside we heard all kinds of noises, stench, language, commands we didn't understand. . . . The doors flung open, and we saw strange uniformed men in striped clothes. They started to yell at us in the Yiddish of Polish Jews: 'Schnell! Raus!' [Hurry, get out!] . . . 'Dort, geht,' [over there] and he pointed towards the flames. We had to move on. So we formed up, true to family tradition, two parents, the oldest sister, and the next sister and the child on my sister's hand. . . . We came up to Mengele, we were standing there. He was pointing left, right. My sister was the first one, with a child, and he pointed to the right. Then my mother, who had a rupture, she had a big belly, she looked like she was pregnant, she wasn't. So I guess that made her go to that side. My father and the two sisters were pointed to his left. He asked my father, 'Old man, what do you do?' He said, 'Farm work.' And then came the next row and the two of us were told also to go after our father and two sisters; and he stopped and he called my father back. 'Put out your hand!' So my father showed him his hand and Mengele smacked him across the face and pushed him to the other side. . . . that's the last we saw of our parents and sister and nephew. It started to get daylight, and we moved on to an area where there was barbed wire on both sides. . . . We were walking, and beyond the barbed wire fences there were piles of rubble and branches, pine tree branches and rubble burning, slowly burning. We're walking by, and the sentries kept on screaming, 'Lauf! Lauf!' [run!] and I heard a baby crying. The baby was crying somewhere in the distance and I couldn't stop and look. We moved, and it smelled, a horrible stench. I knew that things in the fire were moving, there were babies in the fire."

became a nightmare lasting several weeks."[56]

Children were not exempt from such roundups. Operation "Hay Action" in June 1944 involved the kidnapping of forty thousand Polish boys aged ten to fourteen. By that time, 10 million persons, including 3 million prisoners of war, had already been shipped to Germany for forced labor.

Throughout occupied Europe and Russia, the Nazis also plundered whatever

PONDERING THE SS MENTALITY

Filip Mueller, a slave laborer at Auschwitz, had the ghastly task of working in the gas chambers removing bodies for cremation. In his memoir he reflected on a young SS man he saw every day as published in Eyewitness Auschwitz *by Filip Mueller:*

"We [Jewish] prisoners and [SS Sergeant] Stark were worlds apart. For us he seemed to have no human feelings whatever. We only knew him as one who gave his commands brusquely, insulted, abused and threatened us continually, goaded us to work, and beat us mercilessly. To his superiors he was attentive and subservient. I often wondered how it was possible for this young man, scarcely older than myself, to be so cruel, so brutal, harboring so unfathomable a hatred of the Jews. I doubted whether he had actually ever come into close contact with Jews before he came to Auschwitz. He was no doubt a victim of that Nazi propaganda which put the blame for any misfortune, including the war, on the Jews. How was it possible, I often asked myself, for a young man of average intelligence and normal personality to carry out the unspeakable atrocities demanded of him in the belief that thereby he was doing his patriotic duty, without ever realizing that he was being used as a tool by perverted political dictators?"

goods they pleased, enriching Germany at the expense of conquered peoples. Train shipments arriving in Germany carried livestock, foodstuffs, and raw materials, along with priceless art treasures and gold. In the east, where the Germans sought their lebensraum, the Nazis evicted tens of thousands of estate owners and farmers and gave the property to German settlers.

Terror and barbarism had descended across Europe and Russia amid a Nazi empire that Hitler boasted would last a thousand years. But one problem still remained for Hitler and the Germans: They had not won the war. And now, an ever-growing number of armies from all over the world were rallying to smash this empire.

6 Fighting the Whole World

Chapter

Hitler's armies never fully recovered from the severe beating they took during the Russian winter of 1941. Hitler had blundered badly by ordering three simultaneous offensives toward Moscow, Stalingrad, and Leningrad. Although several of his most experienced generals had warned him against this move, Hitler was no longer listening to anyone's advice. He wanted his orders fulfilled, no matter how impossible, impractical, or illogical.

For a time, the entire German front had teetered on the verge of collapse as division upon division of well-equipped Russian soldiers materialized out of nowhere and attacked. Following the Moscow debacle, Hitler had taken over day-to-day management of the army, tossing aside some of the world's finest military experts, the same generals who had engineered the lightning-quick victories over Poland and France. In their place, Hitler looked over the maps and made vital strategic decisions on his own. He also made all of the diplomatic decisions and in December 1941 made perhaps his greatest single blunder.

AMERICA ENTERS THE FIGHT

On Sunday morning, December 7, 1941, the Japanese, who were allied with the Germans, attacked the U.S. naval base at Pearl Harbor, Hawaii. The next day, responding to the devastating air raid which killed over twenty-four hundred sailors and wounded another thousand, the United States and Britain both declared war on Japan.

By this time, Germany and Japan, along with Fascist Italy, had entered into an agreement known as the Tripartite Pact, pledging to provide mutual military assistance in the event one of them was attacked by a nation not already involved in the war. Hitler had also given personal assurances to the Japanese foreign minister that Germany would assist Japan if war broke out between America and Japan.

Remarkably, the Japanese had not informed Hitler they were going to attack Pearl Harbor. Nevertheless, after the attack, Hitler appeared before the Nazi Reichstag and plunged Germany into war against America, giving a long speech on December 11 in which he ridiculed President Franklin Roosevelt and praised the Japanese attack:

National Socialism came to power in Germany in the same year as Roosevelt was elected President. . . . While an unprecedented revival of economic life, culture and art took

President Franklin Delano Roosevelt signs a declaration of war against Germany in December 1941. Roosevelt devoted almost all U.S. military resources to defeating the Nazis.

place in Germany under National Socialist leadership, President Roosevelt did not succeed in bringing about even the slightest improvement in his own country. . . . The fact that the Japanese Government, which has been negotiating for years with this man, has at last become tired of being mocked by him in such an unworthy way fills us all, the German people and, I think, all other decent people in the world, with deep satisfaction.[57]

Reacting to Hitler's declaration of war, the U.S. Congress immediately declared war against Germany with President Roosevelt stating, "Never before has there been a greater challenge to life, liberty and civilization."[58] From this point onward, Roosevelt would devote nearly 90 percent of U.S. military power toward the defeat of Hitler. The Nazis had taken on the world's largest industrial nation, whose war-making potential they scarcely understood. Hitler thought it would take at least a year for America to equip and train an army that could pose a threat to him. He also expressed a low opinion of Americans as soldiers, boasting that German soldiers were naturally superior.

Now, as 1942 began, problems were mounting for Hitler. He had to contend with three principal opponents, Britain, America, and Russia, whose reservoir of manpower and war production capacity dwarfed Nazi Germany's and those of its allies. Making matters worse for Hitler, the war in Russia had already cost him a quarter of his troops and thousands of tanks and planes. The German armed forces were thinly spread throughout Russia, Europe, and North Africa. There, the next major setback for Hitler occurred.

COPING WITH AN INFALLIBLE COMMANDER

After the war, General Alfred Jodl, a principle military aide, revealed that Hitler refused to take any advice from his command staff, as noted in Hitler: The Man and the Military Leader *by Percy Ernst Schramm:*

"Hitler was willing to have a working staff that translated his decisions into orders . . . but nothing more. . . . [He] resented any form of counsel regarding the major decisions of the war. He did not care to hear any other points of view; if they were even hinted at he would break into short-tempered fits of enraged agitation. Remarkable—and, for soldiers, incomprehensible—conflicts developed out of Hitler's almost mystical conviction of his own infallibility as leader of the nation and of the war. . . . The man who succeeded in occupying Norway before the very eyes of the British Fleet with its maritime supremacy, and who with numerically inferior forces brought down the feared military power of France like a house of cards in a campaign of forty days, was no longer willing, after these successes, to listen to military advisers who had previously warned him against such overextensions of his military power. From that time on, he required of them nothing more than the technical support necessary to implement his decisions, and the smooth functioning of the military organization to carry them out."

Hitler studies a map while his command staff awaits his next decision.

DESERT DEFEAT

Twice, since the beginning of the war, in Norway and in France, the British had landed ground troops to challenge Hitler's armies, only to withdraw hastily when it appeared they were doomed to defeat. The next opportunity came in North Africa where troops forming the British Desert Army landed to prevent the Germans from occupying Egypt and possibly conquering the entire Middle East.

To fend off the British, the Germans sent General Erwin Rommel, a blitzkrieg expert, to direct the newly formed Afrika Korps, featuring two armored divisions and a motorized infantry division. At first it seemed as if blitzkrieg had come to the desert. Beginning on May 27, 1942,

the Germans, aided by their Italian allies, staged a lightning attack, surging through the British defenses, causing another hasty British retreat. The battered British wound up at the village of El Alamein, about sixty-five miles from the Suez Canal.

To finish off the British and seal a victory that would bring Hitler control of the entire Mediterranean region, Rommel needed troop reinforcements and supplies. When his Afrika Korps arrived on the outskirts of El Alamein poised to strike the British, Rommel had just 125 operational tanks. Incredibly, Hitler denied Rommel's request, preferring to save all of his resources for large-scale offensives he planned in Russia. Hitler was now obsessed with achieving victory in Russia and dismissed the strategic im-

In 1942 British troops led by General Bernard Law Montgomery (left) defeated German units under General Erwin Rommel (right) and prevented the Nazis from taking control of Egypt.

portance of conquering the Middle East. As a result, Rommel's troops were forced to hold their positions on the outskirts of El Alamein. In his war journal, Rommel criticized the decision:

> When one comes to consider that supplies and materiel [military equipment] are the decisive factor in modern warfare, it was already becoming clear that a catastrophe was looming on the distant horizon for my army. The British were doing all they possibly could to gain control of the situation. With wondrous speed, they organized the shipment of fresh troops into the Alamein position. . . . Our one and only chance to overrun the remains of the British Eighth Army and occupy the east Egyptian desert at a stroke was irretrievably lost.[59]

Just as they had done at Dunkirk, the British were quick to capitalize on Hitler's tactical blunder. They rushed soldiers, tanks, artillery, and ammunition to the troops in El Alamein. At the end of August, Rommel, ever the aggressor, tried to seize the momentum and attacked El Alamein using his limited resources. He was confronted by a well-equipped British army led by a bold new commander, General Bernard Law Montgomery, a man every bit as aggressive as Rommel.

Montgomery launched an all-out counterattack on October 23, 1942. It began at night with a massive artillery barrage that demolished the German defenses. British tanks and infantry then smashed through the German lines, pushing what remained of the Afrika Korps into a headlong retreat, stretching over seven hundred miles.

THE AMERICANS ARRIVE

Complicating matters for the Germans in North Africa, on November 8, a large naval armada landed there, bringing the first contingent of American combat troops into the war, led by General Dwight D. Eisenhower. French forces in the region, loyal to their pro-Nazi government back in Paris, put up light resistance, then caved in and cooperated with the Americans.

The unexpected American landing stunned Hitler and his military staff. To prevent the Allies from sweeping to victory in North Africa, Hitler rushed in reinforcements, but it was too late. By now, Allied warships and planes had seized control of the Mediterranean. They isolated the Afrika Korps by cutting off their supply lines. As a result, the Afrika Korps and all of the reinforcements, totaling 248,000 men, were captured by Montgomery and by American tank commander General George S. Patton. Rommel, who was not captured, never forgave Hitler for the debacle in North Africa.

For the British and Americans, this victory was an important milestone, marking the first time Hitler's troops had ever been ousted from an area they once controlled. In Britain, Winston Churchill commented, "This is not the end, no it is not even the beginning of the end, but it is perhaps the end of the beginning."[60]

To his command staff, Hitler acknowledged the loss of North Africa as a setback, but his primary objective still remained the defeat of Russia, which he believed would mean victory in the war. To achieve this, he now plunged his armies into a gigantic offensive to capture the city that bore the name of

Russia's leader, a place that would symbolize the beginning of Nazi Germany's downfall—Stalingrad.

THE ROAD TO STALINGRAD

Hitler's new strategy was to focus his efforts in the region of southern Russia known as the Caucasus. His objective was to capture the oil fields that fueled Russia's war machinery, thereby disabling it and bringing Russian resistance to an abrupt end. He also wanted to capture the city of Stalingrad, the region's major rail junction and industrial center, located along the Volga River.

To launch this ambitious assault, the German army, which had lost over a million men in Russia thus far, was boosted by the addition of fifty-two non-German divisions recruited from Hitler's allies, including Hungary, Romania, Italy, Slovakia, and Spain. By mid-July, 1942, this combined fighting force had made steady progress. Despite stiff Russian opposition, it was within reach of its two principal objectives, the oil fields in the Caucasus and Stalingrad.

At this point, given his rather limited resources, Hitler needed to decide which of the two main objectives his armies should accomplish. Initially, Hitler leaned toward taking the oil fields. Therefore, he sent one tank army (Fourth Panzer) southward away from Stalingrad to aid another tank army (First Panzer) which was already approaching the oil fields.

However, after ordering this maneuver, Hitler changed his mind. Realizing that the Russians had left Stalingrad virtually undefended, and that he had missed a golden opportunity, Hitler turned the Fourth Panzer Army around and sent it back toward Stalingrad. However, by the time the mechanized army had wheeled around, Russian troops had set up defenses south of the city and were able to block the Panzer tanks. Nevertheless, Hitler insisted he wanted Stalingrad captured and, at the same time, wanted the oil fields taken.

Hitler's general staff and field commanders were utterly dismayed. Hitler was again ignoring their advice, insisting the Russian army was near collapse. Indeed, Hitler had entered a new phase in his conduct of the war. Not only was he ignoring his military experts, he was beginning to ignore reality itself. General Franz Halder, a top military aide, described one revealing scene:

> Once, when a quite objective report was read to him showing that, still in 1942, Stalin would be able to muster from one to one-and-a-quarter-million fresh troops in the region north of Stalingrad and west of the Volga, not to mention half a million men in the Caucasus, and which provided proof that Russian output of front-line tanks amounted to at least 1200 a month, Hitler flew at the man who was reading with clenched fists and foam in the corners of his mouth and forbade him to read any more of such idiotic twaddle.[61]

Those who disagreed with Hitler, such as Halder, were fired. From then on, Hitler only wanted loyalists such as Generals Alfred Jodl and Wilhelm Keitel around him to carry out any order, no matter how disastrous the consequences.

These decisions proved to be quite fateful: At Stalingrad, Hitler was about to steer the German army into the worst disaster in its history.

BATTLE OF STALINGRAD

Hitler assigned the capture of Stalingrad to the pride of the German military, its Sixth Army, commanded by General Friedrich Paulus. From the outset, there were major obstacles. German troops entering the confines of Stalingrad were used to fighting in open spaces that allowed for effective maneuvering of tanks and motorized infantry. Battle conditions in Stalingrad were exactly the opposite. The maze of city streets and tall buildings made battle maneuvers difficult. Heavy aerial bombings by the German air force, combined with intense artillery barrages, turned much of Stalingrad into rubble, blocking streets and creating endless nooks and crannies hiding Russian soldiers.

The battle of Stalingrad became a ferocious street fight in which the Germans paid with blood for every inch they gained. A German lieutenant on the scene wrote:

The street is no longer measured by meters but by corpses. . . . Stalingrad is no longer a town. By day it is an enormous cloud of burning, blinding smoke; it is a vast furnace lit by the reflection of the flames. And when night arrives, one of those scorching, howling, bleeding nights, the dogs plunge into the Volga [River] and swim desperately to gain the other bank. The nights of Stalingrad are a

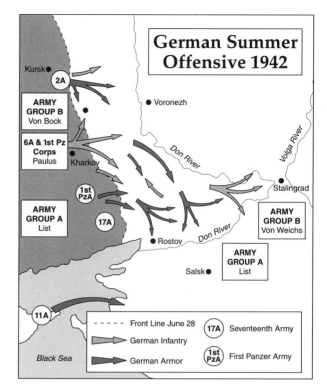

terror for them. Animals flee this hell; the hardest stones cannot bear it for long; only men endure.[62]

As the German death toll mounted, Hitler plunged more divisions into the fight. Meanwhile, the Russians poured nearly a million soldiers into the battle as Stalin told his soldiers, "You can no longer retreat. . . . There is only one road, the road that leads forward. Stalingrad will be saved by you, or wiped out with you."[63]

Outside the city, German troops pushed forward to the banks of the Volga River, cutting off supply lines into Stalingrad. With Russian troops now isolated in the city, the Germans pushed harder than ever. Soon, only a small pocket of Russian resistance remained in Stalingrad. Hitler was confident the city would fall at any moment.

Soviet soldiers take cover in the Red October factory from German fire during the battle of Stalingrad. Despite subzero temperatures and certain defeat, Hitler refused to withdraw his troops from Stalingrad.

And then the Russians struck back. At dawn on November 19, 1942, amid a raging blizzard, thirteen Russian armies that had massed north and south of Stalingrad blasted German lines to the rear of the city. By sending so many troops into Stalingrad, Hitler had weakened his rear defenses, leaving his troops vulnerable. In just three days, the Russians surrounded Stalingrad, trapping the Sixth Army.

Instead of allowing his Sixth Army to try piercing the Russian lines to escape Stalingrad, Hitler ordered the troops to stay put and continue fighting. His plan was to supply the besieged army by airdrops while relief troops, led by Field Marshal Fritz Manstein, fought their way toward Stalingrad. But the plan failed from the start. German planes could not drop enough supplies, and Manstein's troops got to within only thirty miles of the city.

Several of Hitler's generals now pleaded with him to allow the Sixth Army to attempt a breakout to link up with Manstein, their last hope of survival. Hitler was told of the appalling conditions in Stalingrad where thousands of wounded, starving German soldiers were freezing to death amid the subzero temperatures. "I won't go back from the Volga!"[64] Hitler shouted at his generals. Stalingrad was to be held at all costs.

DEMISE OF THE SIXTH ARMY

Before launching their final assault on the besieged Germans, the Russians offered a chance for surrender. On January 8, 1943, three Russian officers carrying a white flag presented surrender terms to General Paulus, who was inclined to accept them. But Hitler forbade Paulus from surrendering. As a result, the Russians blasted the remaining Germans in Stalingrad with five thousand artillery guns.

By January 24, the Sixth Army, lacking ammunition and food, had been reduced to two narrow pockets in Stalingrad. Once more, the Russians offered a chance for surrender. General Paulus sent a personal plea to Hitler: "Army requests immediate permission to surrender in order to save lives of remaining troops."[65]

Hitler responded: "Surrender is forbidden. Sixth Army will hold their position to the last man and the last round and by their heroic endurance will make an unforgettable contribution toward the establishment of a defensive front and the salvation of the Western world."[66]

As the hard-hitting Russians closed in on Paulus and his command staff, Hitler bestowed dozens of last-minute promotions, hoping this would inspire them to

In the aftermath of the battle of Stalingrad, the ninety-one thousand surviving soldiers of the Sixth Army were sent to war camps in Siberia. Only five thousand survived the ordeal.

RUSSIAN HATRED FOR NAZIS

The extraordinary cruelty of Hitler's army troops and SS men while waging their "war of annihilation" in Russia created a furious hatred that enveloped the Russian army. This sentiment is revealed in a 1942 Soviet newspaper article entitled "The Justification of Hatred," reprinted from The Third Reich: A New History:

"This war is unlike former wars. For the first time our people face not men but cruel and vile monsters, savages equipped with every technically perfected weapon, scum acting according to rule and quoting science, who have turned the massacre of babies into the last word of state wisdom. Hatred has not come easily to us. . . . We hate the Nazis because we love our country, the people, humanity. In this lies the strength of our hatred and also its justification. . . . We hate every Nazi for being the representative of a man-hating principle, we hate him for the widows' tears, for the crippled childhood of the orphans, for the pitiable hordes of refugees, for the trampled fields, for the annihilation of millions of lives."

Russia's decision to send the survivors of Stalingrad to Siberia was the result of a deep-seated hatred of the Nazis.

go down in a blaze of glory. Paulus himself was promoted to field marshal by Hitler, realizing no German field marshal had ever allowed himself to be captured.

On January 30, 1943, ten years to the day that Hitler had come to power in Germany, Russian soldiers banged on the door of the Sixth Army's command bunker in Stalingrad. Paulus and his surviving officers quietly surrendered, ignoring Hitler's order that they fight to the last man as well as his implied desire that they commit suicide rather than surrender.

AFTERMATH OF STALINGRAD

Out of an original force of 285,000 soldiers making up the Sixth Army at Stalingrad, 91,000 had survived the battle. They were marched off to begin years of captivity in Russian prisoner-of-war camps in bitter cold Siberia. Only 5.000 would manage to survive the ordeal. After his surrender, Field Marshal Paulus turned against Hitler and Nazism. He collaborated with the Russians, forming a National Committee for Free Germany, and issued radio broadcasts from Moscow urging German troops to surrender. The refusal of Paulus to die honorably in battle, or by his own hand, had enraged Hitler who exclaimed:

> How can one be so cowardly? I don't understand it. . . . What is life? Life is the Nation. The individual must die anyway. Beyond the life of the individual is the life of the Nation. . . . So many people have to die, and then a man like that besmirches the heroism of so many others at the last minute. He could have freed himself from all sorrow and ascended into eternity and national immortality, but he prefers to go to Moscow![67]

On February 3, 1943, a special radio announcement informed the German people they had lost the battle of Stalingrad. The news had a devastating impact. For the first time in the history of Nazi Germany, a shadow had been cast on its future. Even Hitler's most fanatical supporters realized a turning point had been reached.

Twice now, at Stalingrad and before that Moscow, Hitler had waged a furious battle to defeat Russia, only to fail. Hundreds of thousands of German soldiers had been killed fighting a relentless foe that only seemed to be growing stronger. A secret opinion survey taken by the Nazi intelligence service reported:

> People ask, above all, why Stalingrad was not evacuated or relieved, and how it is possible, only a few months ago, to describe the military situation as secure. . . . Fearing that an unfavorable end to the war is now possible, many compatriots are seriously thinking about the consequences of defeat.[68]

Among the Germans a nagging sense of uncertainty had permanently set in. Among the oppressed peoples of occupied Europe and Russia, an inkling of hope sprouted that Hitler's Nazi regime could be brought to an end.

7 The Downfall of Nazi Germany

Beset by a dwindling supply of manpower and ever-increasing Allied aerial and ground attacks, the once mighty German military machine slowly began to unravel. The war of conquest Hitler had launched in 1939 had now evolved into a struggle to save Nazi Germany itself from annihilation.

Above all, the Germans feared the colossal Russian army steadily inching its way toward Germany from the east. After the fall of Stalingrad, German troops in Russia had managed to regroup and go on the defensive but were continually losing ground. In summer 1943, Hitler decided to gamble for victory one last time in Russia, and stave off disaster for Nazi Germany.

KURSK: THE GREAT GAMBLE

At Kursk, located in eastern Ukraine, a half-million Germans stood ready to attack a Russian force nearly twice their size. The daring battle plan involved sweeping around the Russians in two great circling maneuvers and then attacking inward to break them apart. The strategy was reminiscent of the early days of Operation Barbarossa when huge Russian formations were surprised by motorized German troops, then surrounded and captured.

This time, however, there were significant problems. First, the Russians were fully aware of the pending attack. Secondly, the Russian army of 1943 was a far cry from the disorganized rabble the Germans had nearly beaten two years earlier. Realizing the strength of the Russian army, some of Hitler's generals even suggested postponing the offensive altogether. Making matters worse for the Germans, there were delays in the delivery of badly needed equipment to the troops at Kursk. This, combined with last-minute indecision by Hitler over whether or not to give the final go-ahead, pushed the launch date back to July 5. By that time, the Russians were ready and waiting.

Over the next two weeks, one of the largest battles of World War II occurred as 1.5 million soldiers, 6,000 tanks, and 4,000 planes clashed near Kursk. The original German plan for quickly encircling the Russians met with little success. In the southern zone of the offensive, the Germans unexpectedly encountered a formation of 850 Russian tanks. The Germans gathered up 600 tanks of their own, and the two sides blasted away in the largest tank battle of the war. There was no conclusive victor, and both sides rushed in reinforcements just to maintain their positions. Thus far, the battle had cost the Germans 70,000 soldiers, nearly 3,000 tanks and 1,400 planes, losses that were virtually irreplaceable.

At this point, however, Hitler was confronted by an enormous new problem. British and American troops had landed on the island of Sicily, off the coast of Italy, opening a whole new front in the war. Reacting to this development, Hitler disengaged his troops from the Battle of Kursk to preserve his critically low resources.

Seizing the momentum, the Russians began a general advance along a thousand-mile front. By the end of 1943, Russian troops would be at the borders of Poland,

Romania, and Czechoslovakia. Meanwhile, Hitler still needed to figure out what to do about Italy and the new southern front.

HITLER LOSES AN ALLY

The British Eighth Army, led by General Bernard Law Montgomery, along with the U.S. Seventh Army, led by General George S. Patton, began the conquest of Sicily on July 10, 1943. Most of the four hundred thousand soldiers defending the island were Italians, reluctant warriors who had been drafted into the army of Italy's dictator, Benito Mussolini. Confronted by Patton's and Montgomery's tanks, the Italians surrendered in droves. About ninety thousand Germans, aided by Italians who did not surrender, challenged the Allied advance, but wound up evacuating the island and withdrawing to the Italian mainland.

The Allied arrival on Sicily triggered the downfall of Mussolini, who had ruled Italy with an iron fist for two decades. Mussolini's opponents, dismayed that he had plunged Italy into the war on Hitler's side, had him thrown in jail. A new government was then formed which sought an armistice with the Allies. On September 8, 1943, the news became official: Italy, once a staunch ally of Nazi Germany, had surrendered unconditionally. The next day, Allied troops landed on the coast of Italy at Salerno, south of Naples.

By now, however, German reinforcements from Russia and elsewhere had rushed in and occupied about two-thirds of Italy, including Rome. Led by Field Marshal Albert Kesselring, they established a potent defensive line south of Rome, effectively halting the northward advance of British and American troops. By sending in his troops, Hitler temporarily stabilized the situation in Italy. Mussolini was even rescued from prison by a special SS detachment and instructed by Hitler to restore fascism in Italy. In other places, however, Hitler's fortunes were literally sinking.

BATTLE OF THE ATLANTIC

From the moment Britain declared war on Germany in 1939, German U-boat submarines, under the command of Admiral Karl Doenitz, had roamed the North Atlantic and the coast of England, zipping torpedoes through the water and sinking British vessels. Utilizing their "wolf pack" technique, U-boat groups effectively hunted down hundreds of convoys bound for England from America.

By March 1943 the U-boat fleet, now four hundred strong, had nearly severed Britain from its American lifeline. By this time, they had sunk over two thousand ships, killing tens of thousands of merchant seamen and sailors. However, just when it appeared the Germans might win the battle of the Atlantic, newly developed antisubmarine weapons came into use. Radar devices were installed on convoy ships that could pinpoint the positions of far-off U-boats. Long-range American B-24 bombers then attacked the U-boats from air bases in Britain. Aircraft carriers also escorted the convoys and launched fighter planes that machine-gunned the U-boats. Land-based British fighters, equipped with new rocket bombs, attacked as well.

The wolf packs began suffering heavy losses whenever they attacked. By mid-

A German U-boat comes under attack from American B-24 bombers. These bomber planes were instrumental to the efforts of the Allies to retake control of the Atlantic.

1943, the increasing toll caused Admiral Doenitz to withdraw his U-boats from the North Atlantic. British prime minister Churchill later commented, "The only thing that ever really frightened me during the war was the U-boat peril. . . . I was even more anxious about this battle than I had been about the glorious air fight called the Battle of Britain."[69]

With the shipping lanes from America now wide open, Britain became a gigantic arsenal. By mid-1944, 1.5 million soldiers, over four thousand ships, and eleven thousand warplanes had been assembled to invade northern Europe and open up a third front against Hitler.

D-DAY INVASION

Most of Hitler's generals thought the Allies would invade in May or June 1944 and land at Calais, the narrowest distance between the south of England and

OPERATION OVERLORD

London

ENGLAND

Dover

Southampton   Portsmouth   Shoreham

Portland

Calais

Boulogne

PAS DE
CALAIS

Channel

BRITISH   CANADIAN   BRITISH

U.S.

U.S.

English

Dieppe

Le Havre

Cherbourg   UTAH   OMAHA   GOLD   JUNO   SWORD

FRANCE

Carentan

Bayeux

Sto-Lo   Caen

NORMANDY

BRITTANY

Allied Forces
German Mines
0   50
Scale of Miles

a thousand vessels carrying Allied combat troops approached the Normandy coast, taking the Germans by surprise. Following a relentless bombardment by Allied warships and planes, two armies stormed five beaches along a fifty-mile front. The American First Army attacked the western shores of Normandy at beaches code-named Utah and Omaha. The British Second Army attacked toward the east at Gold, Juno, and Sword beaches.

At first, Hitler's generals believed the Normandy landings were just a ruse and that the main invasion would still be at Calais. Two divisions of Panzer tanks remained on standby until the generals realized their blunder and asked Hitler for permission to rush reinforcements to Normandy. However, Hitler hesitated, telling them he preferred to wait until the situation became clearer. Hitler, a night owl by nature, then went to bed.

While Hitler slept, American troops overcame stiff opposition from German gunners at Omaha and Utah. British and Canadian troops, meeting less resistance, broke free of their beaches and headed inland. The German generals, realizing the situation had become critical, tried again to get Hitler's permission to utilize their reserves. But all calls to Hitler went answered until 3 P.M. when the supreme commander finally awoke. At that point he gave the go-ahead and told his commanders the whole Allied invasion "must be cleaned up by not later than tonight."[70] Quite the opposite occurred. By the end of that day, nearly 150,000 soldiers had

the coast of France. There they positioned the bulk of their troops, fifteen infantry divisions, to keep watch. Other troops were stationed at Normandy, considered a less likely landing point.

Despite weeks of good weather, May was quiet. At the beginning of June, a powerful storm moved in, bringing rain, wind, and heavy seas to the English Channel. The Germans were sure the bad weather had postponed any invasion plans. Field Marshal Erwin Rommel, commander of the coastal defenses, even left the area and drove back to Germany to visit his family.

Unknown to the Germans, American general Dwight D. Eisenhower had chosen June 5 as D-day (designated day) for the invasion. The bad weather did indeed postpone the invasion, but only for one day. Beginning at dawn on June 6, 1944, come ashore. Within a week, the number swelled to 500,000.

When the Germans finally rushed in reinforcements, they were blasted by long-range naval guns and ripped apart by Allied warplanes. Given all they were up against, a few of Hitler's top generals decided the time had come to have a talk with their supreme commander about the possibility of saving their troops and Germany itself from certain destruction.

AN AMERICAN ON D-DAY

On the morning of June 6, 1944, American soldier Felix Branham climbed into a landing craft with the rest of Company K of the 116th Infantry Division and headed for Omaha Beach on the coast of Normandy. He recalled what happened, excerpted from June 6, 1944: The Voices of D-Day:

"I got out in water up to the top of my boots. People were yelling, screaming, dying, running on the beach. Equipment was flying everywhere. Men were bleeding to death, crawling, lying everywhere, firing coming from all directions. We dropped down behind anything that was the size of a golf ball. Col. Canham, Lt. Cooper, and Sgt. Crawford were screaming at us to get off the beach. I turned to say to [fellow soldier] Gino Ferrari, 'Let's move up, Gino,' but before I could finish the sentence, something spattered all over the side of my face. He'd been hit in the face and his brains splattered all over my face and my stuff. I moved forward, and the tide came on so fast it covered him, and I no longer could see him."

American soldiers land on Omaha Beach on the coast of Normandy on June 6, 1944.

Running Out of Time

Hitler was now fighting a losing war on three fronts. In the east, German troops were withering in the face of an unstoppable Russian colossus. In the south, Allied troops were slowly advancing up the mainland of Italy and had liberated Rome. In the west, tank columns led by General Patton were roaring toward Germany so rapidly they risked running out of fuel.

Staring at obvious defeat, Hitler's generals wanted to prevent the destruction of Germany by opening peace negotiations with the Allies. However, the problem remained—what to do about Hitler? First, they tried talking to him. Field Marshals Rommel and Rundstedt met with Hitler and informed him that Allied superiority in the air, seas, and on land had made the struggle hopeless. The time had come to bring the war to an end. Hitler disputed this and instead spoke of new super weapons just developed including jet planes and self-propelled bombs that soon would sweep the Allies from the sky and bring the collapse of Britain.

Realizing their supreme commander would never surrender, Rommel and several of Hitler's most senior generals decided to topple him from power. On July 20, 1944, an army officer named Claus Schenk von Stauffenberg carried a time-delayed bomb in his briefcase into Hitler's military headquarters. He placed the briefcase under the conference table near Hitler and left. The bomb exploded, but the heavy oak table shielded Hitler and he was only injured. With Hitler still alive, the coup collapsed and the conspirators wound up shot or hanged. In addition, the Gestapo and SS rounded up thousands of people thought to pose a threat to Hitler, allowing him to rule once again with absolute authority. Now, despite everything, Hitler decided to gamble for victory again, this time against the Americans.

Battle of the Bulge

To the great surprise of his generals, Hitler ordered a bold new offensive in the west. Beginning on December 16, 1944, fourteen infantry and five Panzer tank divisions attacked in a maneuver reminiscent of the brilliant blitzkrieg assault four years earlier that had overwhelmed France.

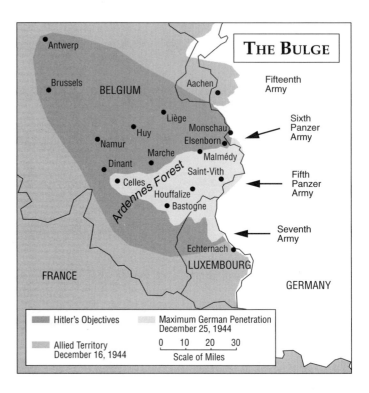

German soldiers advance into Belgium during the Battle of the Bulge. The surprise attack forced American soldiers into a panicked retreat, but they quickly reorganized to rout the Nazis.

Stunned American troops fell into disorderly retreat, with many killed or captured, including a mass surrender of seventy-five hundred soldiers. An American eyewitness recalled the chaos:

> Aid stations overflowing, wounded men being evacuated by Jeep, truck, ambulance, anything that could roll, walking wounded . . . vehicles off the road, mired in mud or slush or damaged by gunfire . . . signal men trying to string wire to elements to cut off or repair [communication] lines which were being shot out as fast as they were put in.[71]

The unchecked German advance created a fifty-mile bulge in the American defensive lines which gave the battle its name. The Germans were aided by several days of foggy weather that grounded the all-powerful American air force.

Unlike 1940, however, when the Germans broke through the French lines and roared northward, this time they stalled due to a variety of logistical problems and stiffening Allied resistance. On December 22 the skies finally cleared allowing Allied warplanes to blast German troop positions all along the bulge. Reinforcements, including Patton's Third Army, arrived and began to counterattack. By January 7, 1945, the battle was all over. Nearly thirty thousand German soldiers, most of them teenagers fresh from the Hitler Youth, had been killed. American casualties included about one hundred soldiers shot in cold blood by SS troops after their surrender.

Surviving German soldiers rushed home to take defensive positions in

Germany to fend off the British and Americans. Meanwhile, in the east, the Russians launched a vast new offensive involving over three hundred divisions. Within weeks they were a hundred miles from Berlin and closing in on Adolf Hitler.

THE DEMISE OF HITLER

In mid-January 1945, after his defeat in the Battle of the Bulge, Hitler moved into a well-fortified underground bunker in Berlin. Here, Hitler held daily military briefings and listened to gloomy reports of the unstoppable Allied advance into Germany. By now, Hitler had sunken into a state of deep despair, punctuated by emotional tirades in which he blamed the collapse of Nazi Germany on his generals and on the weakness of the German people themselves.

In March, Hitler told his minister of armaments, Albert Speer, "If the war is lost, the German nation will also perish. . . . There is no need to take into consideration the basic requirements of the people. . . . Those who will remain after the battle are those who are inferior; for the good will have fallen."[72] He wanted all of Germany's industrial and agricultural resources obliterated by Speer, leaving nothing behind for the invading Allies or surviving Germans. Realizing the madness of this order, Speer ignored it.

Isolated in besieged Berlin, Hitler was losing his mind, issuing frantic orders to nonexistent armies. He was also losing his grip on power. In April he was betrayed by his longest-serving comrades, Hermann Göring and Heinrich Himmler, both of whom attempted, but failed, to take over the leadership of Germany. With the desertions of Göring and Himmler and the Russians advancing deep into Berlin, Hitler prepared for his own demise.

Late in the evening of April 28 he dictated his last will and a political testament expressing many of the same sentiments he originally stated in *Mein Kampf* back in 1924. He blamed the Jews for everything, including World War II, and made a veiled reference to the gas chambers, describing them as a "humane means" of having the Jews atone for the guilt of causing the war. Hitler then married his longtime companion Eva Braun. Champagne was brought out and the few remaining staff members listened to Hitler reminisce about days gone by. Meanwhile, the Battle of Berlin raged above him. A German tank officer on the scene wrote in his diary:

> We retreat again under heavy Russian air attacks. Inscriptions [I see] on house walls [say]: "The hour before sunrise is darkest" and "We retreat but we are winning." . . . The night is fiery red. Heavy shelling. Otherwise a terrible silence. . . . Women and children huddling in niches and corners and listening for the sounds of battle. . . . Nervous breakdowns.[73]

By the afternoon of April 29, Soviet ground forces were a mile away from Hitler's bunker. The last bit of news from the outside world ever to reach Hitler told of the death of downfallen Italian dictator Benito Mussolini, who had been executed by Italian freedom fighters, then hung upside down, and thrown into the gutter.

At noon, April 30, Hitler attended his last military conference and was told the Russians were just a block away. Hitler

A BROKEN HITLER

In late April 1945, with Berlin under siege from the Russian army, young German officer Siegfried Knappe entered Hitler's underground bunker. He later described the scene in his book Soldat: Reflections of a German Soldier, 1936–1949:

"After about forty-five minutes, the meeting in the briefing room ended. Hitler emerged, followed by Dr. Goebbels, General Krebs, General Weidling, and some other people. I saluted, and Hitler walked toward me. As he neared, I was shocked by his appearance. He was stooped, and his left arm was bent and shaking. Half of his face drooped, as if he'd had a stroke, and his facial muscles on that side no longer worked. Both of his hands shook, and one eye was swollen. He looked like a very old man, at least twenty years older than his fifty-six years. Weidling presented me to Hitler: 'Major Knappe, my operations officer.' Hitler shook my hand and said, 'Weidling has told me what you are going through. You have been having a bad time of it.' . . . Hitler said good-bye, shook my hand again, and disappeared in the general direction of Goebbels' quarters. Although his behavior had not been lethargic, his appearance had been pitiful. Hitler was now hardly more than a physical caricature of what he had been. I wondered how it was possible that in only six years, this idol of my whole generation of young people could have become such a human wreck. It occurred to me then that Hitler was still the living symbol of Germany—but Germany as it was now. In the same six years, the flourishing, aspiring country had become a flaming pile of debris and ruin."

At the time this photo was taken, nearly one month before his death, Hitler was in a deep depression over Germany's impending defeat.

and his wife Eva bid a final farewell to remaining military aides and staff, then went back into their private quarters. Several moments later a gunshot was heard. Hitler's aide Martin Bormann and Propaganda Minister Joseph Goebbels entered and found the body of Hitler sprawled on the sofa, dripping with blood from a gunshot to his right temple. Eva Braun had died from swallowing poison. As Russian artillery shells exploded nearby, the bodies were carried up to the chancellery garden, doused with gasoline and burned while Bormann and Goebbels gave a final Nazi salute. The charred remains were then dumped into a shell hole and buried.

SURRENDER OF NAZI GERMANY

At 10 P.M. on May 1, a nationwide radio announcement informed the German people Hitler had died heroically fighting the Russians in Berlin. His designated successor was to be Admiral Karl Doenitz, the famed U-boat commander. Doenitz now presided over a nation in ruins and an army collapsing on all fronts.

On May 5, Admiral Hans von Friedeburg traveled to General Eisenhower's headquarters at Reims, France, to negotiate a general surrender. He was joined by General Alfred Jodl. The Germans hoped to stall the proceedings long enough to allow more troops to flee from the Russians and surrender to the Americans, considered less hostile. Eisenhower, realizing their ploy, demanded the Germans quit stalling and sign an unconditional surrender.

In the early morning hours of May 7, after receiving authorization from Doenitz,

General Jodl signed the official surrender document. The signing was, as Winston Churchill put it, "the signal for the greatest outburst of joy in the history of mankind."[74] Large crowds gathered to rejoice in London, Paris, New York, and Moscow.

For the first time since September 1939, the guns across Europe were silent. Nazi Germany, which had existed for twelve years, was finished. Hitler's war had cost the lives of nearly 7 million Germans, including 3 million soldiers. His chief opponent, Soviet Russia, had suffered staggering losses, including 7 million soldiers and an estimated 16 million civilians. Much of Europe's cultural heritage, including thousand-year-old cathedrals and countless historical and artistic treasures, had also been obliterated.

The magnitude of Nazi barbarism and its tragic human toll had become apparent when Russian, American, and British soldiers liberated concentration camps and saw gas chambers, ovens, piles of ashes, and stacks of dead bodies. After his visit to Ohrdruf near the concentration camp Buchenwald, General Eisenhower commented, "I never dreamed that such cruelty, bestiality, and savagery could really exist in this world! It was horrible."[75]

For the victorious Allies, the question of justice now arose. Fortunately, the rapid demise of Nazi Germany had resulted in the wholesale capture of gigantic archives from all branches of Hitler's government along with secret papers, conference reports, and private diaries. The Nazis had kept meticulous records of their activities, from mass murder in concentration camps to Hitler's private talks. In addition, captured Nazi officials and high-ranking military officers underwent lengthy interrogations. With all of the evidence at hand, the Allies decided to prosecute surviving Nazi leaders for war crimes. The place chosen for the trial was Nuremberg, the now-ruined city that had once hosted annual rallies glorifying Hitler and Nazism.

WAR CRIME TRIALS

Twenty-two high-ranking Nazis went on trial beginning on November 20, 1945. Among the defendants were Hermann Göring, Foreign Minister Ribbentrop, Generals Keitel and Jodl, and Hans Frank, governor of occupied Poland who aided in the Final Solution. Heinrich Himmler, perhaps the most notorious Nazi after Hitler, had killed himself by swallowing poison while in British custody.

The trial was conducted by a joint American–British-French-Russian military tribunal. The four-count indictment included conspiracy, crimes against peace, war crimes, and crimes against humanity such as murder, extermination, enslavement, persecution on political or racial grounds, involuntary deportment, and inhumane acts against civilian populations.

Most of the defendants claimed they were unknowing pawns of Adolf Hitler or were simply following orders. American writer William Shirer, who had spent

Nazi officials and military officers stand trial in Nuremberg. Of the twenty-two defendants, seven went to prison, three were acquitted, and twelve were hanged.

THE WAR'S END

"During the five terrible years, we could not indulge in simple pleasures that life offers to normal people. All our efforts were directed towards fighting the enemy and surviving. Now, for the first time since September 1, 1939, we could unwind and be normal again—to walk streets without fear of hearing the hated 'Halt!,' without the fear of being rounded up by the Germans and pushed into military trucks. No more 'Achtung, Achtung!' [attention, attention!] coming down from the street loudspeakers. No more ghettos, no more starvation, typhus, gas chambers, *Einsatzgruppen* (killing squads). The intense fear and persecution were over."

several years as a foreign news correspondent in Nazi Germany, went to the trial and looked upon the defendants with amazement:

I had often watched them in their hour of glory and power at the annual party rallies in this town. In the dock before the International Military Tribunal they looked different. There had been quite a metamorphosis. Attired in rather shabby clothes, slumped in their seats fidgeting nervously, they no longer resembled the arrogant leaders of old. They seemed to be a drab assortment of mediocrities. It seemed difficult to grasp that such men, when you had last seen them, had wielded such monstrous power, that [men] such as they could conquer a great nation and most of Europe.[76]

Evidence included hundreds of thousands of incriminating documents, Nazi propaganda films and testimony by participants in the Final Solution such as Auschwitz commandant Rudolf Hoess. Also shown were Allied films of the camps depicting emaciated, disease-ridden survivors. Other evidence included the shrunken head of a concentration camp inmate and tattooed human skin used to make lampshades and other household articles.

Seven of the defendants, including Hitler Youth leader Baldur von Schirach, received lengthy prison terms. Three of the defendants were acquitted. The rest were sentenced to death by hanging. In the early morning of October 16, 1946, Ribbentrop was hanged first, followed by Keitel and the others. Two hours before his scheduled hanging, Hermann Göring swallowed poison somehow smuggled into his prison cell. The bodies were burned in the crematory at Dachau, with the ashes scattered in a nearby river.

Twelve additional Nuremberg trials were held from 1946 to 1949, presided by American judges. The Doctors' Trial targeted SS doctors who had operated centers that killed sick and disabled Germans, including five thousand children. Also targeted were leaders of the *Einsatz* killing squads and pro-Nazi corporate leaders. With the passage of time, however, interest in such trials diminished. Many of the convictions were voided in 1951 when a liberal pardon policy went into effect. Overall, only a tiny percentage of those involved in implementing the Final Solution or waging Hitler's war of conquest ever paid a penalty for their actions.

Two Germanys

After the war, traditional European powers such as Britain and France saw their influence wane as two new superpowers emerged—the United States and Soviet Russia. The wartime alliance between America and Russia withered after Hitler's defeat, then dissolved into a long era of mutual distrust known as the Cold War. Postwar Germany found itself in the middle of the dispute, literally divided between the two superpowers.

East Germany, invaded by the Russians during World War II, became a Communist country dominated by Soviet Russia. In the west, where the Americans had invaded, a free market democracy was encouraged, and West Germany became an independent nation allied with the United States.

The demise of Soviet Russia in the late 1980s gave Germans an opportunity to reunite their country. From 1990 onward, Germany has maintained a steadfast commitment to democracy while struggling with the economic stresses brought on by merging wealthier Germans in the west with their much poorer eastern neighbors.

The beginning of the twenty-first century saw the gradual passing of the generation that either participated in, witnessed, or fought against the Nazi reign of terror. Although the perpetrators from the time of Hitler are mostly gone, the mentality that propelled them to murderous action—racial intolerance, lust for power, and economic greed—remains a problem for the world today.

Notes

Chapter 1: The Rise of Hitler

1. Adolf Hitler, *Mein Kampf*. Boston: Houghton Mifflin, 1971, p. 206.

2. Hitler, *Mein Kampf*, p. 224.

3. Hitler, *Mein Kampf*, p. 355.

4. Hitler, *Mein Kampf*, p. 370.

5. Hitler, *Mein Kampf*, p. 497.

6. Quoted in William L. Shirer, *The Rise and Fall of the Third Reich*. New York: MJF, 1990, p. 68.

7. Quoted in John Toland, *Adolf Hitler*. New York: Doubleday, 1976, p. 158.

8. Quoted in Joachim C. Fest, *The Face of the Third Reich: Portraits of the Nazi Leadership*, New York: Pantheon, 1970, p. 32.

9. Quoted in Toland, *Adolf Hitler*, p. 290.

Chapter 2: Bloodless Conquest: Hitler's Gangster Diplomacy

10. Quoted in Robert Payne, *The Life and Death of Adolf Hitler*. New York: Barnes & Noble, pp. 251–52.

11. Quoted in Shirer, *The Rise and Fall of the Third Reich*, p. 194.

12. Quoted in J. Noakes and G. Pridham, eds., *Nazism: A Documentary Reader:* Vol. 1 *The Rise to Power 1919–1934*. Exeter, UK: University of Exeter Press, 1997, p. 186.

13. Quoted in The History Place, "The Triumph of Hitler: Nazis March into the Rhineland," 2001. www.historyplace.com/worldwar2/triumph/index.html.

14. Quoted in Shirer, *The Rise and Fall of the Third Reich*, p. 292.

15. Quoted in Alan Bullock, *Hitler: A Study in Tyranny*. New York: Konecky & Konecky, 1962, p. 345.

16. Quoted in Noakes and Pridham, *Nazism: A Documentary Reader*. Vol. 3 *Foreign Policy, War and Racial Extermination*, p. 683.

17. Quoted in Shirer, *The Rise and Fall of the Third Reich*, p. 326.

18. Quoted in Shirer, *The Rise and Fall of the Third Reich*, p. 329.

19. Quoted in The History Place, "The Triumph of Hitler: Nazis Take Austria," 2001. www.historyplace.com/worldwar2/triumph/index.html.

20. Quoted in Shirer, *The Rise and Fall of the Third Reich*, p. 392.

21. Quoted in The History Place, "The Triumph of Hitler: Conquest at Munich," 2001. www.historyplace.com/worldwar2/triumph/index.html.

22. Quoted in Klaus P. Fischer, *Nazi Germany: A New History*. Continuum: New York, 1995, p. 433.

23. Quoted in Shirer, *The Rise and Fall of the Third Reich*, p. 449.

24. Quoted in Shirer, *The Rise and Fall of the Third Reich*, p. 454.

25. Quoted in The History Place, "The Triumph of Hitler: Nazis Take Czechoslovakia," 2001. www.historyplace.com/worldwar2/ triumph//index.html.

Chapter 3: Blitzkrieg: The Lightning War

26. Quoted in Shirer, *The Rise and Fall of the Third Reich*, p. 530.

27. Quoted in Shirer, *The Rise and Fall of the Third Reich*, p. 532.

28. Quoted in The History Place, "The Triumph of Hitler: The Last Days of Peace," 2001. www.historyplace.com/worldwar2/tri-

umph/ index.html.

29. Quoted in John Pimlott, ed., *Rommel In His Own Words*. London: Greenhill, 1994, p. 147.

30. Quoted in Shirer, *The Rise and Fall of the Third Reich*, p. 599.

31. Quoted in Shirer, *The Rise and Fall of the Third Reich*, p. 645.

32. Quoted in Harold Faber, *Luftwaffe: A History*. New York: The New York Times Book Company, 1977, p. 46.

33. Quoted in David Divine, *The Nine Days of Dunkirk*. New York: W.W. Norton, 1959, p. 115.

34. Quoted in Ernest R. May, *Strange Victory: Hitler's Conquest of France*. New York: Hill and Wang, 2000, p. 446.

35. Quoted in Roy Jenkins, *Churchill: A Biography*. New York: Farrar, Straus and Giroux, 2001, p. 621.

36. Quoted in John Pimlot, *The Historical Atlas of World War II*. New York: Henry Holt, 1995, p. 56.

Chapter 4: Quest for Lebensraum: The Fateful Attack on Russia

37. Hitler, *Mein Kampf*, p. 383.

38. Quoted in Shirer, *The Rise and Fall of the Third Reich*, p. 830.

39. Quoted in Pimlot, *The Historical Atlas of World War II*, p. 80.

40. Quoted in Laurence Rees, *War of the Century: When Hitler Fought Stalin*. New York: New Press, 1999, p. 44.

41. Quoted in Shirer, *The Rise and Fall of the Third Reich*, p. 854.

42. Quoted in Ian Kershaw, *Hitler: 1936–1945: Nemesis*. New York: W.W. Norton, 2000, p. 391.

43. Quoted in Shirer, *The Rise and Fall of the Third Reich*, p. 854.

44. Quoted in Pimlot, *The Historical Atlas of World War II*, p. 86.

Chapter 5: Absolute Power— Absolute Terror

45. Quoted in Milton Meltzer, *Never to Forget: The Jews of the Holocaust*. New York: Harper & Row, 1976, pp. 52–53.

46. Quoted in Noakes and Pridham, *Nazism: A Documentary Reader: Vol 2 State Economy and Society 1933–1939*, p. 496.

47. Quoted in Guido Knopp, *Hitler's Holocaust: Decision*. Mainz, Germany: ZDF Television, 2000.

48. Quoted in Noakes and Pridham, *Foreign Policy, War and Racial Extermination*, p. 933.

49. Quoted in Noakes and Pridham, *Foreign Policy, War and Racial Extermination*, p. 933.

50. Quoted in Michael Berenbaum, *The World Must Know: The History of the Holocaust as Told in the United States Holocaust Memorial Museum*. New York: Little, Brown, 1993, p. 118.

51. Quoted in Yitzhak Arad, *The Pictorial History of the Holocaust*. New York: Macmillan, 1990, p. 174.

52. Quoted in The History Place, "Holocaust Timeline," 1997. www.historyplace.com/world war2/holocaust/timeline.html.

53. Quoted in The History Place, "Holocaust Timeline," 1997.

54. Quoted in Rudolf Hoess and Steven Paskuly, *Death Dealer: The Memoirs of the SS Kommandant at Auschwitz*. New York: Da Capo, 1996, p. 27.

55. Quoted in Berenbaum, *The World Must Know*. p. 134.

56. Quoted in Michael Burleigh, *The Third Reich: A New History*. New York: Hill and Wang, 2000, p. 552.

Chapter 6: Fighting the Whole World

57. Quoted in Shirer, *The Rise and Fall of the Third Reich*, pp. 898–901.

58. Quoted in *Page One: The Front Page*

History of World War II as Presented in the New York Times. New York: Galahad, 1996, p. 50.

59. Quoted in Pimlott, *Rommel in His Own Words,* p. 119.

60. Quoted in Jeremy Issacs, *The World at War.* London: Thames Television, 1972.

61. Quoted in Shirer, *The Rise and Fall of the Third Reich,* p. 917.

62. Quoted in C.L. Sulzberger and Stephen Ambrose, *American Heritage New History of World War II.* New York: Viking, 1997, p. 247.

63. Quoted in Pimlot, *The Historical Atlas of World War II,* p. 114.

64. Quoted in Sulzberger and Ambrose, *American Heritage New History of World War II,* p. 247.

65. Quoted in Shirer, *The Rise and Fall of the Third Reich,* p. 930.

66. Quoted in Shirer, *The Rise and Fall of the Third Reich,* p. 930.

67. Quoted in Shirer, *The Rise and Fall of the Third Reich,* p. 933.

68. Quoted in Noakes and Pridham, *Nazism: A Documentary Reader.* Vol 4 *The German Home Front in World War II,* p. 543.

Chapter 7: The Downfall of Nazi Germany

69. Winston S. Churchill, *Memoirs of the Second World War.* Boston: Houghton Mifflin, p. 410.

70. Quoted in Shirer, *Rise and Fall of the Third Reich,* p. 1038.

71. Quoted in Rupert Butler, *Hitler's Young Tigers.* London: Sheridan, p. 152.

72. Quoted in Pimlot, *The Historical Atlas of World War II,* p. 200.

73. Quoted in Sulzberger and Ambrose, *American Heritage New History of World War II,* pp. 552–53.

74. Quoted in Sulzberger and Ambrose, *American Heritage New History of World War II,* p. 559.

75. Dwight D. Eisenhower, *Letters to Mamie.* New York: Doubleday, 1978, p. 248.

76. Shirer, *The Rise and Fall of the Third Reich,* p. 1142.

For Further Reading

David A. Adler, *Child of the Warsaw Ghetto.* New York: Holiday House, 1995. Fictional account of life in the Warsaw Ghetto, the uprising against the Nazis, and imprisonment in Auschwitz told through the eyes of a Jewish boy.

Michael Berenbaum, *The World Must Know: The History of the Holocaust as Told in the United States Holocaust Memorial Museum.* Boston: Little, Brown, 1993. Utilizing the museum's artifacts, photos, and eyewitness testimonies, this book skillfully documents and explains the Holocaust.

Bruce Bliven Jr., *From Casablanca to Berlin.* New York: Random House, 1965. A simply written, easy-to-read account of World War II in Europe, from the Allied landings in North Africa to the surrender of Germany.

Don Nardo, *Adolf Hitler.* San Diego: Lucent, 2003. A clear and easy-to-read biography of the Austrian who rose from obscurity to power as the leader of the Nazi Party and, later, the German Nation.

John Pimlot, *The Historical Atlas of World War II.* New York: Henry Holt, 1995. Chronicles the major and minor battles of the war using over one hundred maps. A very interesting and easy-to-use resource.

Elie Wiesel, *Night.* New York: Bantam, 1960. The 1986 Nobel Peace Prizewinner gives a terrifying account of the death camp horrors he experienced as a young boy with his father. This book is one of the most powerful accounts ever written concerning the Holocaust.

Web Sites

The History Place. (www.historyplace). Comprehensive time lines with primary source documentation, informative text, and hundreds of photos, assembled by the author of *World War II in Europe.*

The Nuremberg War Crimes Trials. (www.yale.edu/lawweb/avalon/imt/imt.htm). A large collection of the legal documents, evidence, and testimonies used to bring Nazis to justice.

Roosevelt's Speeches and Fireside Chats. (www.fdrlibrary.marist.edu). Features an archive of the inspiring words Roosevelt spoke to the American people during his presidency.

The United Stated Holocaust Memorial Museum. (www.ushmm. org.) Contains a wealth of information including personal histories, a photo archive, and current information about the museum and its educational mission.

Works Consulted

Books

Yitzhak Arad, *The Pictorial History of the Holocaust.* New York: Macmillan, 1990. An extraordinary compilation of four hundred photos from Yad Vashem (the Holocaust Martyrs' and Heroes Remembrance Authority in Jerusalem) and from private collections, providing haunting proof of Hitler's Final Solution.

Gerald Astor, *June 6, 1944: The Voices of D-Day.* New York: St. Martin's, 1994. Over seventy first-person accounts of D-day by surviving veterans.

Alan Bullock, *Hitler: A Study in Tyranny.* New York: Konecky & Konecky, 1962. This was the first complete biography of the German dictator and remains one of the most authoritative and readable accounts of his rise and fall.

Michael Burleigh, *The Third Reich: A New History.* New York: Hill and Wang, 2000. Filled with human and moral considerations missing from more traditional accounts, this examination of Nazi Germany gives full weight to the experiences of ordinary people during the twelve-year Reich.

Winston S. Churchill, *Memoirs of the Second World War.* New York: Bonanza Books, 1959. A fascinating abridgment of Churchill's six-volume history of the war.

David Divine, *The Nine Days of Dunkirk.* New York: W.W. Norton, 1959. This book discusses the forced retreat of Allied troops in 1940.

Deborah Dwork and Robert Jan van Pelt, *Auschwitz: 1270 to the Present.* New York: W.W. Norton, 1996. Shows how an ordinary prewar town in Poland was transformed step-by-step with diabolical thoroughness into Nazi Germany's most lethal killing center.

Dwight D. Eisenhower, *Letters to Mamie.* New York: Doubleday, 1978. Despite his high-profile position as supreme allied commander, Eisenhower was a rather private man. This collection of letters he wrote to his wife from Europe during World War II reveals both the ordinary and extraordinary characteristics of the man.

Eric Joseph Epstein and Philip Rosen, *Dictionary of the Holocaust: Biography, Geography and Terminology.* Westport, CT: Greenwood, 1997. This concise resource features two thousand entries, essential for an accurate understanding of the personalities, places, and major events of the Holocaust.

Harold Faber, *Luftwaffe: A History.* New York: The New York Times Book Company, 1977.

Joachim C. Fest, *The Face of the Third Reich: Portraits of the Nazi Leadership.* New York: Pantheon, 1970. Contains insightful profiles of leading figures including Hitler, Göring, Goebbels, and Himmler, along with background information revealing the overall significance of each man.

Klaus P. Fischer, *Nazi Germany: A New History*. Continuum: New York, 1995.

Martin Gilbert, *The Day the War Ended: May 8, 1945, Victory in Europe*. New York: Henry Holt, 1995. Hour by hour, place by place, this book recounts the final dramatic moments of World War II.

Adolf Hitler, *Mein Kampf*. Boston: Houghton Mifflin, 1971.

Rudolf Hoess and Steven Paskuly, *Death Dealer: The Memoirs of the SS Kommandant at Auschwitz*. New York: Da Capo, 1992. Hoess admits to being history's worst mass murderer, personally supervising the extermination of over 2 million persons, mostly Jews, at Auschwitz. This is the first complete translation of his memoirs into English, providing insight into the mentality of this genocidal man and valuable information about the Nazi SS hierarchy.

Roy Jenkins, *Churchill: A Biography*. New York: Farrar, Straus and Giroux, 2001. The story of the man who always believed he was destined to play a great role in the life of Britain.

Ian Kershaw, *Hitler: 1889–1936: Hubris*. New York: W.W. Norton, 1998. This first installment of a two-part biography by the noted British historian covers the period from Hitler's birth in 1889 through Germany's reoccupation of the Rhineland in 1936. Kershaw used historical documents previously unavailable, including Russian archives, to create this important new biography.

———, *Hitler: 1936–1945: Nemesis*. New York: W.W. Norton, 2000. The second installment of Kershaw's two-part biography covers the war itself and Hitler's downfall.

Ernst Klee et al., *The Good Old Days: The Holocaust as Seen by Its Perpetrators and Bystanders*. New York: Konecky & Konecky, 1991. A collection of diaries, letters, and confidential reports written by the executioners and sympathetic observers involved in the Holocaust, illustrated with "souvenir" photos they took.

Siegfried Knappe with Ted Brusau, *Soldat: Reflections of a German Soldier, 1936–1949*. New York: Dell, 1992. Provides a unique glimpse into the Nazi war machine as seen by an eager young officer who participated in nearly every major military campaign.

Milton Meltzer, *Never to Forget: The Jews of the Holocaust*. New York: Harper and Row, 1976. Explores the human stories behind the statistics of the Holocaust, allowing the men, women, and children who lived through the terror to describe it in their own words.

Ernest R. May, *Strange Victory: Hitler's Conquest of France*. New York: Hill and Wang, 2000.

Bernard Law Montgomery, *The Memoirs of Field-Marshal and the Viscount Montgomery of Alamein.* Cleveland: World, 1958. Britain's most famous commander during World War II chronicles his military career.

Filip Mueller, *Eyewitness Auschwitz.* New York: Stein and Day, 1979. The first-person account of a slave laborer who worked in the gassing installations, witnessing families, whole townships, and cities of Jews put to death and burned to ashes.

J. Noakes and G. Pridham, eds., *Nazism: A Documentary Reader.* Exeter, UK: University of Exeter Press. This four-volume set provides a wealth of primary source documentation covering Hitler's rise to power, Nazi Germany's economy and society, foreign policy, war and racial extermination, and the German home front during the war.

Robert Payne, *The Life and Death of Adolf Hitler.* New York: Barnes & Noble.

John Pimlott, ed., *Rommel In His Own Words.* London: Greenhill, 1994. One of the best-known and most successful commanders of World War II reveals his philosophy of war and detailed information about major battles he engineered. Includes photos taken by Rommel.

Laurence Rees, *War of the Century: When Hitler Fought Stalin.* New York: New Press, 1999. Based on the BBC television series of the same name, this companion book makes good use of compelling eyewitness accounts and a fascinating selection of photos.

Percy Ernst Schramm and Donald S. Detwiler, ed., *Hitler: The Man and the Military Leader.* Chicago: Academy Chicago, 1981. A unique analysis of Hitler by his official war diarist.

William L. Shirer, *Berlin Diary.* New York: Alfred A. Knopf, 1941. The daily insights of an American radio correspondent as he watched Hitler take Germany down the road to war in the last half of the 1930s.

————, *The Rise and Fall of the Third Reich.* New York: MJF, 1990. This is still the best overall history of Hitler's Germany, written by an American journalist who was there until late 1940, watching Hitler and witnessing many important events. After the war, Shirer spent over five years sifting through Nazi documents to write this definitive history.

John Toland, *Adolf Hitler.* New York: Doubleday, 1976. Based on previously unpublished documents, diaries, notes, photographs, and interviews with Hitler's colleagues and associates. Regarded by many as the definitive biography of the Nazi leader.

Dmitri Volkogonov, *Stalin: Triumph and Tragedy.* New York: Grove Weidenfeld, 1991. This was the first major study to come out of Soviet Russia in the era of glasnost (openness), providing answers to the perplexing questions surrounding the mysterious man who ruled Russia for three decades.

Internet Source

George J. Wittenstein, "Memories of the White Rose," The History Place—Points of View, 1997. www.historyplace.com.

Videos

Jeremy Issacs, *The World at War*. London: Thames Television, 1972. The excellent British-made documentary series, notable for the stirring narration by Sir Laurence Olivier, extensive use of Allied and Nazi film footage, and comments from participants such as Albert Speer, Karl Doenitz, and many others, who were still living when the series was originally produced.

Guido Knopp, *Hitler's Holocaust*. Mainz, Germany: ZDF Television, 2000. A six-part German-produced documentary series exploring the legacy of Hitler's attempt to exterminate the Jews.

Laurence Rees, *War of the Century*. London: BBC Television, 1999. Revealing comments from German and Russian soldiers are effectively combined with archival footage to describe history's most lethal conflict, Hitler's attack on Russia.

Index

62–63
Nuremberg Laws and, 64
Poland and, 62, 65, 71
Russia and, 62, 66–68
Wannsee Conference and, 68
see also concentration camps; Jews
Hungary, 55
Hurricane fighter plane, 50

Italy
Allied troops and, 85–86
Britain and, 76
German alliance and, 39, 48
Greece attack and, 54
Mussolini execution and, 92
new southern front and, 86
Tripartite Pact and, 73

Japan, 73
Jenkins, Roy, 49
Jews
anti-Jewish demonstrations and, 17, 64
anti-Jewish propaganda and, 63–64, 72
anti-Semitism and, 18–19
Austrian, 64
book burning incident and, 30
extermination of, 10, 12–13, 53, 66–69
Final Solution and, 69, 95–97
German, 18, 64
Hitler's hatred of, 14–15, 17, 52, 92
Marx and, 53
Nuremberg Laws and, 64
Polish, 65–66
Russian, 66–68
Ukrainian, 66–67
Jodl, Alfred, 75, 79, 94–95
Jungvolk, 22
Juno Beach (code name), 88

"Justification of Hatred, The" (Soviet newspaper article), 82

Kammerling, Walter, 64
Keitel, Wilhelm, 33, 79, 95–96
Keller, Helen, 30
Kesselring, Albert, 86
Kiev (Ukraine), 56, 58, 67
Knappe, Siegfried, 93
Kraków (Poland), 42, 66
Kreisleiter, 22
Kursk (Ukraine), 84–85

Landsberg Prison (Germany), 21, 23
Latvia, 40
"Law for Removing the Distress of the People and the Reich, The," 27
Lebensraum, 52, 59, 72
Lenin, Vladimir, 57
Leningrad (Russia), 55–57, 73
Liverpool (England), 51
Lochner, Louis P., 30
Lodz (Poland), 66
Lok, Alice, 70
London, 50–51, 94
Ludecke, Kurt, 24
Ludendorff, Erich, 19–20, 26
Luftwaffe (German air force), 46–47, 51
Luxembourg, 48

Maginot Line, 43–44
Manstein, Erich von, 59, 80
Marx, Karl, 53
Marxists, 14, 16, 18
Mediterranean (region), 76–77
Mein Kampf (My Struggle) (Hitler), 21, 23, 52, 63, 92
Mengele, Josef, 71
Middle East, 76–77
Molotov, Vyacheslav, 39
Montgomery, Bernard Law, 76–77, 86
Moscow, 56–59, 73, 94
Mueller, Filip, 72

Munich (Germany)
Agreement, 37–38
Beer Hall Rebellion and, 17, 19–21, 26
British air raids on, 51
German Worker's Party and, 16
Nazi Party and, 19
World War I and, 14
Mussolini, Benito, 39, 54, 86, 92

Naples (Italy), 86
Narvik (Norwegian seaport), 45
National Committee for Free Germany, 83
National Socialist German Worker's Party (NSDAP). *See* German Worker's Party
Nazi Party
Blockwart and, 36
book burning and, 30
formation of, 16–19
Gestapo and, 36, 64, 90
government elections and, 21, 23, 25
Great Depression and, 25
Hitler's reorganization of, 22
Hitler Youth and, 22, 91, 96
Kulter and, 30
Nazi, origin of term and, 19
Propaganda Ministry and, 63
racial thinking of, 54
see also swastika
Nazism: A Documentary Reader. Vol.1 State, Economy and Society (Lochner), 30
Nazi-Soviet Nonaggression Pact, 40–42, 52
Night of Broken Glass, 62–63
Nonaggression Pact. *See* Nazi-Soviet Nonaggression Pact
Normandy (France), 88

Picture Credits

About the Author

Philip Gavin is a web publisher who founded The History Place (historyplace.com), visited by millions since 1996. Mr. Gavin has written extensively on the rise of Adolf Hitler and the Holocaust, along with American history topics including the Vietnam War, and world history topics such as the Irish Potato Famine. Mr. Gavin has a background in journalism and television. In 1994, he received an award for "Songs of the Season," a children's holiday special. He lives in Quincy, Massachusetts.